Published by
WOTTON-UNDER-EDGE HIST

BY ASIA TO AUSTRALIA

The Diary of a Voyage in 1849

by

JAMES BROOM

edited by Beryl A. Kingan

2004

"BY ASIA TO AUSTRALIA"

Published by:
Wotton-under-Edge Historical Society
Wotton Heritage Centre
The Chipping
Wotton-under-Edge
Gloucestershire GL12 7AD

Printed by:
Parchment (Oxford) Ltd
Printworks,
Crescent Road,
Cowley,
Oxford OX4 2PB

ISBN 0-9548895-0-9

Contents

Illustrations

One of James's Diary drawings

INTRODUCTION

In a folder labelled Post, among the Wotton-under-Edge Historical Society's records in the Wotton-under-Edge Heritage Centre, was a small notebook, hand-written in pencil. It proved to be the first part of a diary of a voyage to Adelaide, South Australia, in 1849. It had come from 2 Haw Street, Wotton-under-Edge, Gloucestershire, together with various items of Post Office memorabilia and a school exercise book belonging to Elizabeth Foxwell, daughter of the chemist and postmaster, Eusebius Foxwell, and his wife Charlotte. At one time in the nineteenth century their home was also the Post Office.

The notebook had no cover and the end pages were so rubbed as to be almost illegible. The writing was very small, frequently crossed out and alterations inserted. The book consisted of two sections of folded pages sewn together. Perhaps there should have been a second volume, now missing, as the entries stopped before arrival in Adelaide. The last two pages, however, list the officers and crew and the passengers, so possibly the writer, for some reason, did not intend to continue his entries. A few loose pages describe the beginning of his return journey, in 1851.

From internal evidence, described later, it appeared that the writer was called James, he lived in Warminster, Wiltshire, and he was writing the diary for his mother, in Bath. The puzzle was, how did the diary come to be in the former Post Office in Wotton-under-Edge? A possible answer seemed to be that he was Charlotte Foxwell's brother. The 1851 Census had given her birthplace as Bath. The results of research undertaken to confirm or refute this theory are given in the section "James Broom and his Family".

The Reference Librarian at the Mortlock Library of South Australia, in Adelaide, provided copies of the passenger lists in the *South Australian Register* for 19th February 1850, when the *Asia* arrived, and for 9th May 1851, when the *Royal Shepherdess* left Adelaide. The one name common to both lists was Brown, James Brown on the *Asia* and simply Brown on the *Royal Shepherdess*. There was also a William Brown on the *Asia*, and a James McKenzie, but entries in the diary make it clear that neither of these was the writer.

For confirmation of a link with Eusebius and Charlotte Foxwell a copy of their marriage certificate was obtained. It transpired that they married on 2nd July, 1844, not in Bath but in St Luke's Church, Chelsea, Middlesex, by licence. Charlotte's father was James Broom, solicitor, her residence being in the parish of St Luke, Chelsea. The officiating minister was the Revd J S M Kyrle, Rector of Yatesbury, Wiltshire. Yatesbury is near Avebury, between Chippenham and Marlborough, within reasonable distance of Bath. Mr Kyrle had been in Yatesbury for only a few months. The advowson of the living belonged to his family, the Money Kyrles. Previously he had served his first curacy in Alderley, close to Wotton-under-Edge, so Eusebius Foxwell would have known him well. As well as having asked him to officiate at their wedding they later named their son John Kyrle Foxwell.

The passengers on the *Asia* provided their own evening entertainment, and James included the programme of one of their concerts. One item is given by "the celebrated Mr Brown", possibly the William of the passenger list, but two songs are credited to Mr Broom, the name being written fairly clearly. One of the poems James quotes, of which he might himself have been the author, includes the words "M[ortal?] Broom". Could this be a reference to his name? James's writing in the diary is difficult to decipher, so it is feasible that the compilers of the two printed passenger lists in the newspaper misread Brown for Broom, choosing the much more common name. James's list of the passengers, on the back page, is particularly difficult to read. One of the more legible names can be deciphered under magnification as J. Broom, but it is easy to see how it could be interpreted as Brown. Several other names on the various published passenger lists have discrepancies in their spelling.

Evidence for the identity of the diarist, his intended reader and his home town can be found throughout the diary:

Oct 13: His friend and travelling companion, and his friend's father, are named as Charles and Mr Brodribb, of Warminster [Wiltshire].

Oct 18: He compares the market in Plymouth with that in Bath.

Nov 5: He refers to the Bonfire at Warminster.

Nov 10: He looks forward to working in Adelaide and "finding myself between a pair of good traces, and easy collar on".

Nov 12: He describes the coat he is wearing as "the one that clients so much admired at Warminster".

Nov 24: The concert programme includes two songs by Mr Broom and one by the "celebrated Mr Brown". Both names can be found among the passengers.

Dec 1 & 2: He refers to a passenger named Brown in connection with a quarrel, clearly not the diarist himself.

Dec 6: His entry is addressed to his mother, and he makes reference to shopping in Bath.

Dec 23: He addresses "My dear Mother".

It has already been said that the diarist's writing is very small, in pencil, with many alterations and crossings out, and difficult to decipher. Additionally his spelling is idiosyncratic, sometimes phonetic, and his punctuation often non-existent. Many words are illegible. In transcribing the diary, therefore, some words have had to be omitted and others guessed. These have been enclosed in square brackets, together with occasional explanations. To improve clarity capital letters at the beginning of sentences and full stops, with occasional commas, have been inserted. This has sometimes entailed a subjective judgement where the sense was ambiguous. Capital letters in other places have been retained. Grammar and spelling have been left as written by James, but in some cases the conventional spelling has been added in square brackets. Later in the diary James appears to have confused dates, and has added a note to the effect that the entry actually belongs somewhere else. Such comments have been retained. His descriptions of his health are somewhat repetitive so not all have been included, and one or two of the poems he quotes have also been omitted. On most days James noted the *Asia's* position, the weather, wind, and distance covered, and named the sails being used. Some has been retained in context, but most of this information has been recorded separately, after the diary section.

"If I cannot obtain a situation in my old trade", James comments, he would be happy to become a Bushman. Evidently his intention was to emigrate but in 1851, less than eighteen months after his arrival, he was on his way back to England. The few pages concerning the return voyage give no clue as to the reason, nor do we know what his old trade might have been, except for the reference to "clients" in Warminster, but he seems to have had a particular interest in the prices of goods, and in opportunities for trade.

REGULAR PACKETS to AUSTRALIA.— EMIGRATION on the NEW PRINCIPLE (established in 1848), to ADELAIDE, PORT PHILLIP, and SYDNEY, taking goods and passengers from the London and Southampton Docks. The fine first-class teak ship ASIA, 643 tons register, 900 tons burden, JOHN ROSKELL, commander, now lying at the Jetty, London Docks, will leave London on the 19th April; Gravesend, on the 22nd April; and Southampton, on the 1st May, with passengers of one class only, at a uniform rate of £21 per adult, bedding and mess utensils included. Children in proportion.—An experienced surgeon has been appointed, who will be accompanied by his family.—For dietary scales and further particulars apply to T. B. Mallet, 4, Castle-court, Birchin-lane; or to HALL (BROTHERS), 3, Leadenhall-street, London.

Newspaper Advertisement
"Daily News" 3 April 1851

EMIGRATION

1849, the year of James Broom's departure for South Australia, was a record year for emigration in general. Murray's Almanack, 1850, records that in 1844 there were 1,114 immigrants arriving in Adelaide, while in 1849 there were 16,166. Some of the reasons are outlined in the section on Warminster. Incentives to leave Britain included assisted passages, both by the Government and by philanthropists and landlords, many of the latter being relieved that tenants would not then become a drain on their resources or on those of the parish. Some large landowners set up funds to assist emigrants, such as the Wiltshire Emigration Association, founded by Lord Ailesbury in 1849. This Association arranged for 258 people from Wiltshire to settle in South Australia and Victoria, before its closure in 1852. There was always the hope that life would be better in a new country, underlined by the sometimes glowing reports in letters of family and friends who had already made the great decision. The prospect of wealth from the gold fields was a special attraction. Altogether emigration had become fashionable.

A Proclamation dated 5th January, 1848, enabled purchasers of waste Crown lands to nominate for a free passage in the emigrant ships three emigrants for every £80 of the purchase money, providing the nominees were eligible according to the regulations. Settlers who had not purchased land could pay a deposit for bringing out relatives, and the Government would defray part of the passage price, even if they were otherwise ineligible. However fertile the land, and rich in natural resources, it would remain undeveloped without the men to work it. Thus those deemed eligible for assisted passages were artisans, agricultural and other labourers, miners, and gardeners, all under 50 years of age, single female domestic servants, widows not over 35 years without children under 12 years old, and the wives and children of married emigrants. They had to have been working at one of these occupations, and intending to continue in that line, of good moral character, in good health, and vaccinated or to have had smallpox. In addition there were emigrants who had paid their own fares, and been approved by the Emigration Agent in England. On arrival they would receive a land order immediately available for those wishing to occupy and cultivate Crown land. It could be used for the purchase of any land after two years' continuous residence in the Colony. James refers to two of the sailors who were working their passage. The information he provides on many of the passengers suggests that they had probably paid their own fare, or had it paid for them, as might have been the case with James himself.

William Harcus, in *South Australia* (1876) refers to a *Handbook for Emigrants* which he had published some years before. As well as the conditions of the Immigration Act already described, he advises the clothing and other luggage that should be provided. The minimum amount allowed for each male over 12 included six shirts, six pairs of stockings, two warm flannel shirts, two pairs of new shoes or boots, two complete suits of strong exterior clothing, four towels and two pounds of marine soap. For each female over 12 six shifts, two flannel petticoats, six pairs of stockings, two pairs of strong boots and shoes, two strong gowns (one of which must be of warm material), four towels and two pounds of marine soap. It would be advisable also for men to take two or three coloured shirts, and, for women and children, an extra supply of flannel. There was a maximum allowance of quantity and weight of luggage, which had to be packed in strong boxes. Anything above that had to be paid for. Certain articles, such as mattresses and feather beds, offensive weapons, spirits, and dangerous articles could not be taken. Harcus suggested that additional yards of cloth and extra shoes or boots would be useful on the voyage. He adds that, "where there are children, a number of cheap caps should be provided, as young people are apt to lose their head-coverings overboard." Passengers were advised to take certain items of food, such as a cheese and a ham, as a change from the ship's diet, and jam for the children. Throughout the diary James comments on the items which he found useful, or otherwise, and suggests others which potential emigrants should add to their lists. Harcus also advises the provision of useful and interesting books, especially school books for their children. Some ships would have had a teacher or two among the passengers, who could set up classes for the children during the three or four months they were on board.

Boxes were brought up from the hold occasionally, during fine weather. The conditions in the hold were not conducive to the preservation of the contents of the boxes. Clothes were mildewed and food often had to be thrown away. Cockroaches, flies and fleas were commonplace.

Some emigrant ships were one class only. On others the accommodation was divided into three, the cabin, the intermediate, and steerage. A plan of the *Asia* shows the arrangement of the cabins below the poop deck. An advertisement for a voyage on that ship in 1851 specifies one class only. The passenger list of the *Royal Shepherdess* illustrates the three divisions. James travelled steerage, as did his friend Charles.

The cabins were partitioned, giving a space six feet by three feet for two people in the married accommodation. A child would have to share it. Single men travelled steerage, together at one end of the ship. Bedding was provided. The bunks also had to be used for the storage of small items. There would be a limited number of lamps below decks, one, locked, being left on all night, the rest had to be out by 10 o'clock. No naked flames of any kind were allowed, and no smoking below decks.

The Passenger Act of 1847 regulated the emigrants' day. They had to rise at 7 am, unless the ship's surgeon gave permission to stay. Breakfast was at 8.0 or 9.0 am, dinner at 1.0 pm and supper at 6.0 pm. All passengers had to be in bed by 10 p.m. Passengers had to roll up their beds, sweep the decks and the space below the beds and throw the dirt overboard, before breakfast. There was a rota of sweepers, males over 14, whose duties included sweeping and cleaning the decks after each meal.

Passengers were divided into groups of six to twelve for meals with one of them elected mess captain. This was James's role, and one of his duties was to make the puddings for his mess. He had to obtain supplies from the stores and see them prepared for cooking, lay the table, wash the tinware, clear the table, and carry away the slops. Passengers were at the mercy of the purser and the cook, who were often disagreeable and dishonest, giving short weight, or refusing to cook the food properly, or at all. Eating utensils and a cooking pot were provided. Assisted immigrants who had behaved well were allowed to keep them. James commented that a watch had to be kept on them or they would be stolen. Theft and drinking were common problems on these ships. James describes a fight between two of the men.

Sheep, pigs and hens were kept on board, the hens in a coop on the deck. This explains the title of one of the poems in James's diary. One of the pigs was to be slaughtered to provide fresh meat for Christmas Day on the *Asia*.

Passengers had to make their own entertainment. One passenger on the *Asia* had brought her piano, which was kept in the cuddy, the officers' cabin, and taken out for concerts and recitals. James played the violin, and was much in demand to accompany dancing. He includes in his diary the programme for one of their concerts, in which he took part. Home entertainment was a feature of family life and many passengers would be prepared to play their part. There was no lack of social life, even shipboard romances, as some of the poems in the diary make clear. On Sundays it was usual for a service to be held, led by the captain, the doctor, or one of the passengers possibly if appropriately qualified or experienced. A sermon might be read, from a book of collected sermons. James describes several of these services, which he appreciated, having been a regular member of one of the chapels in Warminster, although on occasion he was quite critical. Often a group such as the Pastoral Aid Society provided tracts and small books for the emigrants. For many their faith helped them through the discomforts and dangers of the voyage, and provided comfort in illness and even bereavement.

Conditions on the emigrant ships varied greatly, depending largely on the captain, his officers and the crew. With people crowded together in a small space, inadequate ventilation, poor hygiene, lack of fresh water and food, it is not surprising if passengers fell ill, and some died. Measles and whooping cough caused many deaths among children. There seem to have been comparatively few such problems on board the *Asia.*

Just as James was returning from Adelaide on the *Royal Shepherdess*, the *Asia* was again preparing to leave England for Australia. An advertisement in the *Daily News* of 3rd April 1851 announced that "the fine first-class teak ship *Asia*, John Roskell Commander", would be leaving London on 19th April, Gravesend on the 22nd and Southampton on 1st May, with passengers of one class only, at a uniform rate of £21 per adult, bedding and mess utensils included. Did the two ships pass en route, and did James recognise his former home of four months?

Immigration Figures from Murray's Almanack, Adelaide, 1850

Arrivals at Port Adelaide by sea in the 1840s:

1844	1,114
1845	2,336
1846	4,458
1847	5,646
1848	7,664
1849	16,166

During 1849 the arrivals were from:

Great Britain		British Colonies		Foreign States	
Males	Females	Males	Females	Males	Females
6,854	5,647	1,455	583	981	646

A typical barque, such as the *Asia* before her conversion to a ship
Three masts, from stem to stern, foremast, mainmast and mizzen-mast
Sails in ascending order:

Foremast	**Mainmast**	**Mizzenmast**
Foresail	Mainsail	Spanker
Lower fore topsail	Lower main topsail	
Upper fore topsail	Upper main topsail	
Lower fore topgallant sail	Lower main topgallant sail	
Upper fore topgallant sail	Upper main topgallant sail	

Projecting from the bow is the jib-boom, with flying jib, outer jib, inner jib and fore topmast staysail.
Between the foremast and mainmast are the foretopmast studding sail and foretopgallant studding sail, and between the mainmast and mizzenmast are the main top-mast and main top-gallant studding sails, one on each side of the ship in both cases.

In her conversion to a ship the *Asia* would have had the fore and aft sail on the mizzen mast replaced by square sails like those on the other two masts. James describes this work in his entry for 24th November, though some names are different and the *Asia* had an extra sail at the top of both the fore and the main masts.

THE SHIPS

Lloyd's Registers and Lloyd's Lists for the relevant years provide information about the three ships named in the diary, the *Asia*, the *Pandora*, and the *Royal Shepherdess*. Further information comes from the Maritime Museums in Greenwich, Liverpool and South Australia, as well as from the diary itself. *The South Australian Register* newspaper included shipping news.

The *Asia*

No: 841 in Lloyd's Register for 1849, she was a barque of 523 tons. Her Master was John Roskell. She was built of teak in Calcutta in 1815, so was quite an old ship when James sailed in her. Her dimensions were 122ft 3 ins x 30ft 10ins x 5ft 10ins between decks. Although she started as a three masted barque her rigging was changed to that of a ship during that voyage, and she is so described in the information from South Australia Maritime Museum. Her owners in 1849 were Ingram &c. The columns for the port to which she belonged and the destined voyage were left blank in that entry.

In 1850, on a later voyage, she was no: 835, the owners were Hall & Co, the port to which she belonged was London, and the destined voyage was from London to Sydney.

The *Asia* is mentioned three times in Lloyd's List for 1849. On October 11 she left London, bound for Adelaide, South Australia. On October 20 she arrived in Plymouth from London, bound for Port Philip [Sydney]. It was in Plymouth that James joined the ship. There is no entry for her departure from Plymouth, and the Harbour Master recorded only that "several emigrant ships sailed today" [October 24]. The entry date for her arrival off Madeira was November 22. This follows the shipwreck of the *Pandora* on October 29, described by James, illustrating the time lag in communications.

From 1827 the *Asia* had made a number of convict voyages. According to Ian Nicholson, in *Log of Logs*, she had carried 169 female prisoners in 1847. She had been a migrant ship in 1839, with the Captain named as Freeman. Ian Nicholson queries whether in 1851 she was the same migrant ship, with Captain Roskell, sailing from England to Adelaide. This seems probable, considering the growing number of emigrants, rather than convicts, especially in 1849.

A plan of the cabins in the poop, held by the Maritime Museum, Greenwich, shows the two largest cabins, one occupied by the captain, as 12 feet long and 9 feet wide. The poop is the highest part of the ship, at the stern end. Both these cabins are shown as having a WC on the outside, at the stern. The next four, two on each side of the ship, were narrower, 8 feet wide. They each had a WC apparently inside the cabin. Four more cabins, two on each side of the ship, were only 5ft 4ins wide, and 6 feet long. Of these, one on the starboard side was a pantry. The two on the port side were

engines. As well as saving the captain and crew the ship was stripped of everything moveable. The whole operation took two hours. James was not impressed with Captain Smith, "a sad contrast to our own".

On Tuesday, 6th November, the *Asia* arrived off Madeira. James describes the island and the disembarkation of the Pandora's crew the following day. They would have to be in quarantine for five days. For the same reason no-one from the *Asia* was allowed ashore, and she remained anchored off-shore for the same period. However, the opportunity was taken by the Captain to purchase supplies of bread and fruit. This included bananas, which James likened to an English fig, but sweeter, and rather insipid.

The *Royal Shepherdess*

No: 463 in Lloyd's Register for 1849, she was described as a barque of 406 tons, constructed of yellow mahogany, partly from old timbers. Her dimensions were 106ft 9ins x 25ft 0ins x 17ft 4ins.

The Master then was Mr A. Scott, but when James returned from Adelaide in 1851 the Master's name was Bell. She was built in Leith by L. Rose & Son, in 1845 and was passed as A1 in 1848. The owners were Fleming & Co, her port of registration was Glasgow and the destined voyage in 1849 was from London to Ceylon. There is no entry for her in Ian Nicholson's *Log of Logs*.

The *Royal Shepherdess* had left Singapore on December 11 1850. James joined her at Adelaide on May 6 1851 and they sailed on May

9, although her departure is recorded as May 8 in the *South Australian Register* of the next day. The ship was anchored at the North Arm for a few days, before they finally left. On May 19 they turned back to Adelaide as the pumps were not working. This must have revived memories of the *Pandora* in James's mind. On May 24 they were back in port. Whether James continued his return voyage in the *Royal Shepherdess* is not known as his diary finishes with the return to Adelaide. The repairs were apparently successful as there is a further entry on July 1 1852, when, with Master John Bell, she arrived in Port Adelaide having left London, via Deal, on March 11 1852.

JAMES BROOM AND HIS FAMILY

As the diary was one of the items found in the former Post Office in Wotton-under-Edge it seemed a reasonable assumption that the writer was connected with the Postmaster and his wife, who lived in that house. Eusebius and Charlotte Foxwell were married in St Luke's Church, Chelsea, Middlesex, by licence, on 2nd July 1844. According to their marriage certificate Charlotte was resident in that parish and her father was James Broom, solicitor. The 1851 Census for Wotton-under-Edge stated that Charlotte had been born in Bath. The diarist was writing for his mother, who lived in Bath. The supposition was that the writer was Charlotte's brother. However, passenger lists for the outward and return voyages gave his name as James Brown. It was quite possible that, in common with several other passengers, his name had been recorded incorrectly. Evidence within the diary seems to confirm this. James makes no mention of his father, nor any other family members, apart from his mother.

A will was sought for a James Broom of Bath, presuming he had died between Charlotte's wedding in 1844, and James's departure for Australia in 1849. In the event the only will which seemed relevant was indeed for James Broom, Gentleman, of Bath, but it was dated 1st April 1841, with probate granted to his widow, Charlotte, on 8th September 1843. There was no requirement for

Charlotte's marriage certificate to state whether her father was still living, so the earlier date does not rule out that will. The will made provision for Charlotte to bring up their two youngest children, Henry John and Harriet. There was no mention of the older children. James Broom's residence was in the parish of SS Peter & Paul in Bath (Bath Abbey). The 1841 Census shows Henry, aged 13, an Office Boy, and Harriet, aged 8, living in Westgate Buildings with Ellen Robbins, a single woman aged 40, of independent means. In his will James had left £73 to Ellen Robbins for her service to him and his family. Neither his widow, Charlotte, nor any older children appear at that address in the census returns. Charlotte, however, was found as a female servant, one of three, in Grosvenor Buildings, Walcot. A family named Crawford lived at the same address.

The Census took place on the night of 6/7 June 1841. James died on 4th April, shortly after making his will. His death certificate gives his age as 44 and his occupation as Turner. He died of consumption at 4 (or 6) Westgate Buildings, Bath. Ellen Robbins, of the same address, was present at his death, and registered it, signing by mark. As she was apparently unable to read she would not have realised that the registrar had interpreted Attorney as Turner. There is a record of a marriage between James Broom and Elizabeth Robins in Bath Abbey on 16th March 1766, so Ellen might have been a relation.

James referred in his will to a previous covenant concerning his property, that when the tenant's lease expired the property should be sold, and the proceeds used to repay the principal and interest of two mortgagors, Mr Fox of Melksham and Mr Copleton, the remaining money to go to his wife for the upbringing of their two youngest children. The remaining length of the lease might account for the delay in probate, which was granted two years later. James's profession and ownership of property would justify the description of gentleman.

An 1830 Directory for Wiltshire lists James Broom as an attorney with offices in Lowbourne, Melksham, and in Corsham. One of the mortgagors named in his will was Mr Fox, of Melksham. There is an entry in the Directory under Gentry for Mr Wm Fox, esq, of Market Place. Harriet was born in Melksham in 1832, but baptised in Bath, two years later, and the registers show that the family lived in Bath.

Henry, at 13, was an Office Boy although, as the son of a gentleman, it might have been expected that he would still be classed as a scholar. In the 1851 Census Charlotte, James's widow, aged 53, was a midwife and Harriet, now aged 18, a milliner. Charlotte is listed in the 1850 Directory, as a nurse. Her address was given variously as 4, 6 and 7 Westgate Buildings. She is not listed in the 1849 or 1852 Directories, although the diary shows that she was living in Bath in 1849. The Directories would have been compiled the previous year. In the 1861 Census number 4 was uninhabited, and there were no occupants named Broom in numbers 6 and 7.

The 1851 Census states that Charlotte, James's widow, was born in the parish of St James, Westminster, Middlesex. This would have been in 1798. An entry in the parish register for 29th May, 1817, records the marriage of James Broom and Charlotte Hoult.

The parish registers for St Swithin's Church, Walcot, Bath, list the baptisms of their children. James was born on 21st April, 1818, and baptised with Charlotte, born 1819, on 22nd August, 1819. Their father, James, was an Attorney at Law, and the address was Upper Bristol Road. Edward was born on 8th August, 1820, and baptised with Emma, born 18th August, 1821, on 11th January, 1822. Their father was a solicitor, and their address 6 Albion Place.

Harriet was born on 19 July, 1832, and baptised on 10th August 1834. Again James was described as a solicitor, and their address now was Sion Hill.

Henry John does not appear in the baptism register.

The baptism register provides the final evidence that James Broom, the diarist, was the son of James and Charlotte Broom, and brother of Charlotte Foxwell, née Broom.

The entries in the Censuses and the Directories indicate that the family had fallen on difficult times financially. James Broom died of consumption, so would have been ill for some time before his death, and unable to carry on his attorney's practice. Hence Charlotte, his wife, had gone into service, and had to leave her youngest children to the care of Ellen Robbins, who also registered James's death. Later Charlotte moved into Westgate Buildings, where her husband had been living before his death. There she became a nurse and midwife. Henry, who might otherwise have still been at school, was working as an Office Boy. Harriet later became a milliner. In 1851, aged 18, she was living with her mother in Westgate Buildings. Edward and Emma had presumably left home, as they do not appear on the 1841 or 1851 Censuses. Charlotte was possibly in Chelsea, perhaps in service, by the time her father died. The marriage licence, dated 1844, states only that she had been living there for at least fifteen days. James was also away from home, though apparently not yet in Warminster, as he does not appear in the 1841 Census there. James had been able to receive an education, as the diary shows. He quoted poetry from memory, though not always quite accurately, he tried to write poetry himself, he could sing, and he played the violin.

Westgate Buildings in 1841 was largely occupied by professional people, including attorneys, accountants, and commissioners for oaths. Some of the addresses could have been offices, or possibly people working from home. By 1861 there were several single names listed as separate families but under the same house number, in multiple occupation. Westgate Buildings occupies both sides of the street of that name. The ground floor is now converted to a variety of small shops and cafés. The centre of the terrace on one side is part of the City of Bath College. Jane Austen knew Westgate Buildings well. When the Austen family moved to Bath in 1801, after their father's retirement, it was one of the addresses they considered, but they rejected it. She commented, "Though quite in a lower part of the town, they are not badly situated in themselves." *Persuasion* was written in 1815/16 and published posthumously in 1818. Quite possibly James Broom senior had been acquainted with her.

The duplication of names James and Charlotte can be confusing, so a brief family tree has been constructed:

James Broom born 1797 married Charlotte Hoult born 1798

1817
at St James Westminster

Children:

James	born 1818	baptised 21 April 1819 at St Swithin's Walcot Bath to Australia in 1849
Charlotte	born 1819	baptised 21 April 1819 at St Swithin's Walcot married Eusebius Foxwell of Wotton-under-Edge 2 July 1844 at St Luke's Chelsea
Edward	born 1820	baptised 18 August 1821 St Swithin's Walcot
Emma	born 1821	baptised 18 August 1821 St Swithin's Walcot
Henry John	born 1828	
Harriet	born 1832	baptised 10 August 1834 St Swithin's Walcot

Given the long gap between Emma and Henry John possibly there were other children who did not survive or who, like Henry John, do not appear in the baptism register of St Swithin's, Walcot.

WARMINSTER

Warminster, where James had been living prior to his departure for Australia, is a former wool, corn-trading and coaching town in Wiltshire. William Cobbett, in his *Rural Rides* of 1830, described it as "a really nice and good town. It is a great corn-market - one of the greatest in this part of England - and here things are still conducted in the good old fashion". The Corn Exchange was built by the Marquess of Bath in 1850. Until then corn had been sold in the open street. In 1851, at the time of the census, the population was 4220.

The Repeal of the Corn Laws in 1846 and the general agricultural depression during the nineteenth century caused hardship throughout the predominantly rural county. Only a few years before James left it was reckoned that one sixth of the population of Wiltshire was receiving poor relief. From 1815 the price of corn had been kept artificially high, which benefitted landowners, but was to the detriment of their tenants. When the Corn Laws were repealed the landowners suffered, and many tenants were evicted.

New arrangements were made for the giving of relief to the poor. Previously it had been the responsibility of individual parishes. Parishes were now combined into unions with a central workhouse, managed by a Board of Guardians. Instead of receiving out-door relief, the able-bodied poor had to seek, and earn, it in the workhouse. The workhouse in Warminster eventually became the local hospital.

Most unions encouraged poor families to emigrate overseas, and large landowners often provided assistance. This was not entirely philanthropic in motive, as it resulted in the removal from the parish the responsibility of those who might need relief. The Wiltshire Emigration Association was founded in 1849, the year James left, to enable emigration to South Australia and Victoria. Emigration was becoming fashionable, possibly influenced by reports of the discovery of gold in those areas.

James, however, was not alone in deciding to emigrate. He had a friend in Warminster, Charles Brodribb, who accompanied him. J D & U Brodribb were Grocers and Wine Merchants, with a shop in the Market Place of Warminster. An ironmonger's shop also in the Market Place was owned by Charles Brodribb, presumably the father of James's friend, who travelled to Plymouth with his son. James had made his own way to Plymouth, having visited his mother in Bath on the way. Neither James nor Charles appear on the assisted passage lists.

They would probably have travelled by coach at first, perhaps to Westbury. The Wiltshire Somerset and Weymouth Railway, with assistance from the Great Western Railway, had built a line from Chippenham, on the Bristol line, to Westbury in 1848. It was not extended to Warminster until 1850. There was no through line until 1856. James travelled from Bath to Exeter, en route for Plymouth, by train.

James makes several references to Warminster in his diary. On 5 November he remembers the bonfire which would have been lit to commemorate the failure of the Gunpowder Plot of 1605. On 16 December he mentions Cop Heath (properly Cop Heap) on the town's outskirts.

Describing the Independent Chapel in Plymouth, which he attended while waiting for the *Asia* to arrive from London, he says "The building is not of the same denomination or quite so large as that of Warminster, but of similar formation." There were several chapels in Warminster to which he could have been referring, but his name does not appear in any of their records. The Old Meeting had been a Presbyterian Chapel founded in about 1680. It had suffered a split in 1720, when the minister, Dr Bates, was accused of the Arian heresy, denying the doctrine of the Trinity. A Congregational Church, in Common Close, had been built in 1840 on earlier foundations, replacing the "New" or "Lower Meeting". The New Meeting was a Methodist Chapel in George Street, built in 1861 on the site of an 1804 chapel. An Independent Methodist Chapel, in Pound Street, now closed, was built in 1842. A Salvation Army Citadel, in Chapel Street, 1882 - 1976, now demolished, was built as an Independent Methodist Chapel in 1827. Later it was taken over by Congregationalists. A small chapel was built by the Independents in 1802, in Bread Street, chiefly for week-day meetings. A Baptist Chapel was built in 1810. James might have attended any of these. Clearly Sunday observance and worship meant a great deal to him, from his comments on the Sundays throughout his diary.

The shrub Cytisus praecox, with its abundance of creamy-white flowers in spring, is known as Warminster Broom. Perhaps James felt a particular affinity with the town which had been his home.

PLYMOUTH

James arrived in Plymouth by the 1.30 train from Bath, where he had been visiting his mother, via Bristol and Exeter. At Bristol there had been a short break when he was able to buy refreshments. The journey from Bristol to Exeter he described as a "long and tedious ride". It was dark when he arrived in Exeter and he had to stay in an hotel overnight. The following day he continued his journey to Plymouth.

Not knowing Plymouth he decided to join his fellow passengers, Mr & Mrs Fountain, at the hotel to which they had been recommended, the White Horse in Westwell Street. This street ran from Princess Square to the Royal Parade, just west of the Guildhall. The present Law Courts have been built on the site. James also mentions the South Devon Hotel, where they dined and enjoyed the evening's entertainment.

There was delay of a week before the *Asia* arrived from London, en route to South Australia. James and his companions used the time to look around the town, but he commented that they were all "heartily tired of strolling about doing nothing but wear out shoe leather and getting rid of our money".

Each day they walked along to the Quay hoping for news of the *Asia*. Quay Road, in the Barbican area, forms the western edge of the Sutton Pool and leads to the pier known as the Mayflower Steps. From here the Pilgrims sailed in 1620, followed by early settlers in Virginia and emigrants to Australia such as James and his fellow passengers on the *Asia*. The Mayflower Memorial stone was placed there in 1891, and the gateway erected in 1934, so James would not have seen these.

Unlike the city centre the Barbican area partially survived the bombing in 1941 so James would still recognise some of the buildings. They visited the Citadel, built by Charles II, where the soldiers were drilling. On one of the inspection days they watched the soldiers going through a number of field movements. Another time they listened to the band playing there.

Having heard that the band was also going to play at the Barrack Yard in Devonport they walked there and enjoyed the music. They had been to Devonport a few days earlier, to inspect the dockyard with one of the officers as a guide. James considered the dockyard at Portsmouth more worth visiting. As they had some time to wait until they could be taken round they took a boat to visit one of the naval vessels.

A visit to the market, held on Thursdays and Saturdays, passed another hour. James compared the stalls quite favourably on the whole with those in the Bath and London Markets. On the Sunday he and his new friends attended the Independent Chapel. The sermon was good but the singing poor, without musical accompaniment.

Plymouth seems to have been able to provide both good accommodation and entertainment for its visitors.

First Settlement of Adelaide, 1837.
from "South Australia" William Harcus, 1876

Port Adelaide from the Landing Place (Looking across Gawler Reach)" by S T Gill, 1848
Watercolour on paper, 28.2 x 46.1cm.
Gift of the South Australia Company 1890.
Art Gallery of South Australia, Adelaide.

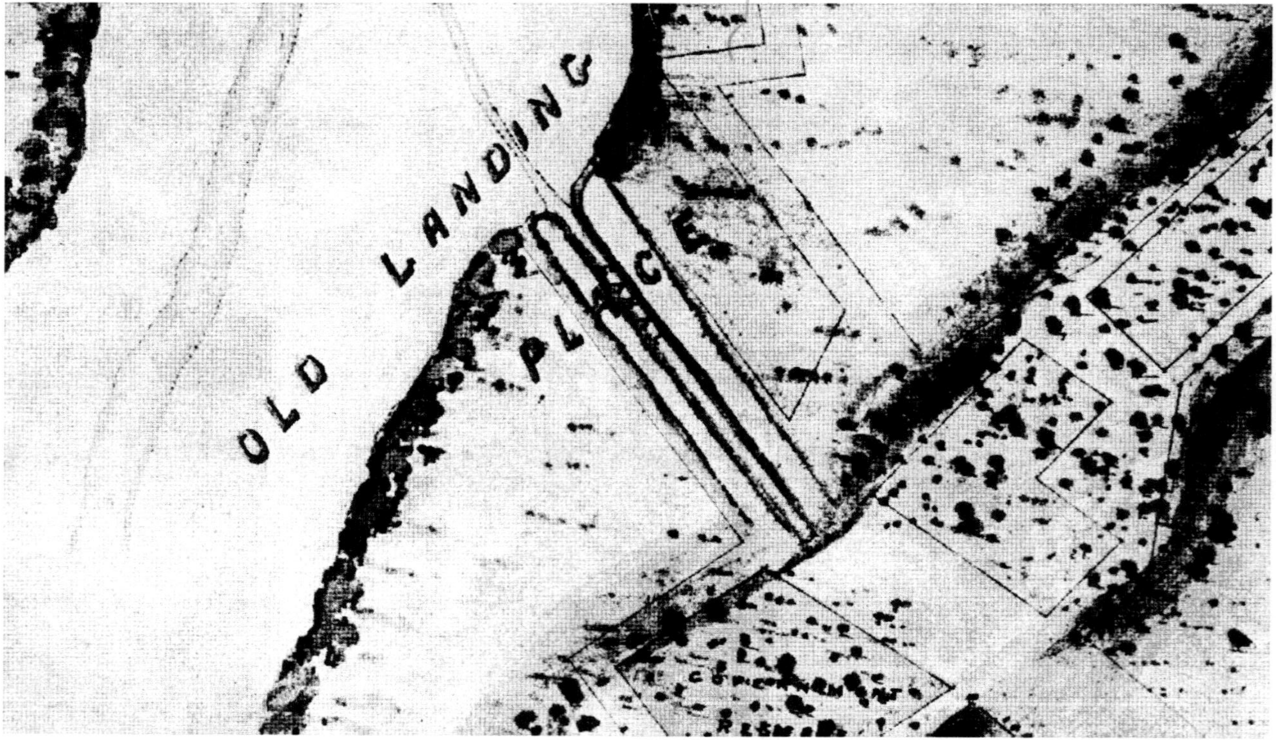

Plan of Old Port, Adelaide,
by G. S. Kingston
Courtesy of the State Library of South Australia: SLSA: C245

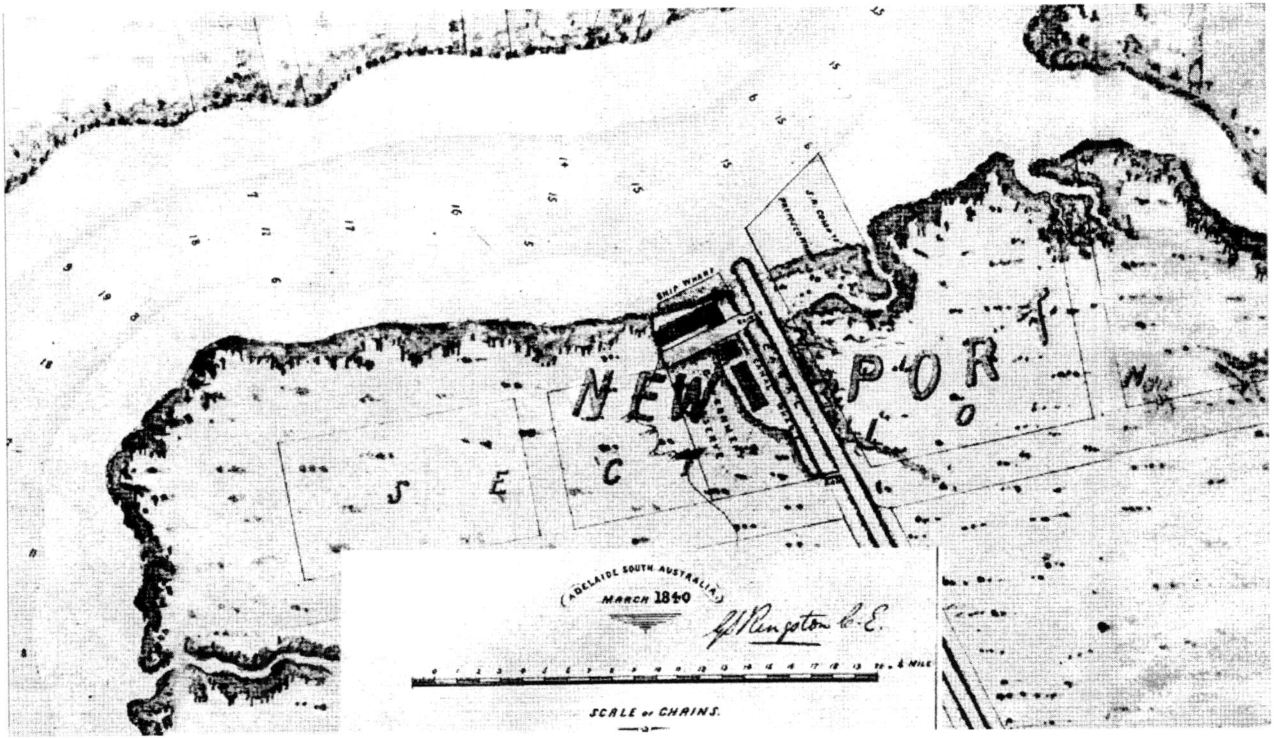

Plan of New Port, Adelaide, 1840
by G. S. Kingston
Courtesy of the State Library of South Australia: SLSA: C245

ADELAIDE

The *Asia* arrived in Port Adelaide on 19 February, 1850, after a voyage lasting four months. Unfortunately the diary ends on 23 December so we do not know what James's reactions might have been on seeing his new home for the first time.

South Australia was founded in 1836. A group of men in London had opened negotiations with the Government in 1831 hoping to obtain a charter giving them certain concessions, but this came to nothing. In 1834 they resumed negotiations, and an Act was passed in August of that year. The conditions included no convicts were to be sent to South Australia, no charge on Britain, and no State church was to to be recognised. The proceeds from the sale of land were to be used to bring out labour from Britain. The Colony was proclaimed in Glenelg, the first settlement, six miles from the future city. A sketch in *South Australia*, edited by William Harcus, which was made in 1837, shows a few wooden houses with steeply pitched roofs, and several tents, in a heavily wooded area. Port Adelaide, eight miles from the city, had its origin in a swamp in a creek, known as Port Creek, about two miles upstream from the present port. It was found to be too shallow and inconvenient, so the port was soon moved. A sketch of 1848 looking across the harbour shows the port much as James would have seen it. Other smaller ports were built around the coast. The Port in 1850 has been described as a poor collection of single storey temporary buildings with shingle roofs.

The city soon grew. Murray's *Almanack* of 1850 gives the population figures for the Adelaide area as 22,390 in March 1846, increasing to 56,450 by December 1849. The *Almanack*'s compiler describes the town and port as "fast losing the primitive appearance of a settlement and very many public and private buildings recently built are already giving them a handsome appearance." There were churches of all denominations, many good shops, and several large houses, now in the care of the *National Trust of South Australia*, which James would have seen. Somewhat incongruously, close to these residences were some poor hovels, as described by one visitor to the city. Adelaide itself had about 12,000 inhabitants. The colony had been divided into counties, of which Adelaide was one, and a legislature had been formed.

A great variety of manufactures had been started. Copper, lead, gold and silver had been discovered, and were being mined. In the mountains were saw mills, taking advantage of the plentiful supply of timber. Land was enclosed and cultivated, and orchards and vineyards planted. Many of the settlers at this time described in their letters home the fertility of the land, and the abundance of fruit and other crops. Vegetables, however, were in short supply, one settler commented, as the people were too busy to grow their own. Beyond Adelaide county boundaries the country was being occupied as sheep and cattle runs. The *Royal Shepherdess*'s cargo list illustrates the growing export of wool.

In the early 1850s gold was discovered in the neighbouring colony of Victoria, in the area around Melbourne. This had a serious effect on Adelaide, as most of the men left for the gold fields. This left a shortage of labour for trade and farming, a shortage of customers, and a shortage of coinage as the men had taken it with them. Trade was bad, and life very difficult for those left behind, until the gold diggers had made sufficient finds to bring the results back home. Melbourne's gain was Adelaide's loss. Could this situation have had some bearing on James's decision to return to England?

On 6 May 1851 James embarked on the *Royal Shepherdess*. In fact the ship did not sail for a few days. He travelled to the port in a carrier's cart, stopping at the first halfway house, four miles away. There were two halfway houses, a quarter of a mile apart, known as the New and the Old Halfway House, the latter having been built twelve years earlier. After heavy rain the road was almost impassable. James took a boat out to the ship, changed into dry clothes, and returned to shore, where he dined at the Railway. The following day he accompanied some of the crew back to shore, as he had some business to deal with, arranging to meet them later at the Commercial Inn, owned by Polly Grey and her third husband. She had apparently gone to Australia as a convict, having arrived in Adelaide from Van Diemen's Land [Tasmania].

It was not until 9 May that the *Royal Shepherdess* left the port to anchor at the North Arm, where they remained for a few more days. This arm of the sea extended inland from Snappers Point for

12 to 14 miles, in width half to three quarters of a mile. James describes the lightship where incoming ships anchored to await the pilot. The lightship was an old French vessel, the *Ville de Bordeaux*, seized by the English in 1840 for smuggling. The crew were lodged at Fordhams, which by James's time was known as the Sturt Hotel, in Adelaide.

At last, on 14 May, the voyage proper commenced, sailing down the Investigator Strait, which lies between Yorke Peninsula and Kangaroo Island. They had hoped to round Cape Leeuwin, at the south western tip of Western Australia, within five or six days, but the state of the ship's pumps necessitated returning to Adelaide for repairs. They had covered about 100 miles at this point. The sight of Kangaroo Island was a relief, although they still had 90 miles to go before reaching Port Adelaide. Finally they arrived at the lightship and were taken in tow by the steam tug to their berth in the port. The last entry on these loose pages was made a few days later, and James gives no further descriptions of Adelaide or the port, any later entries having not survived.

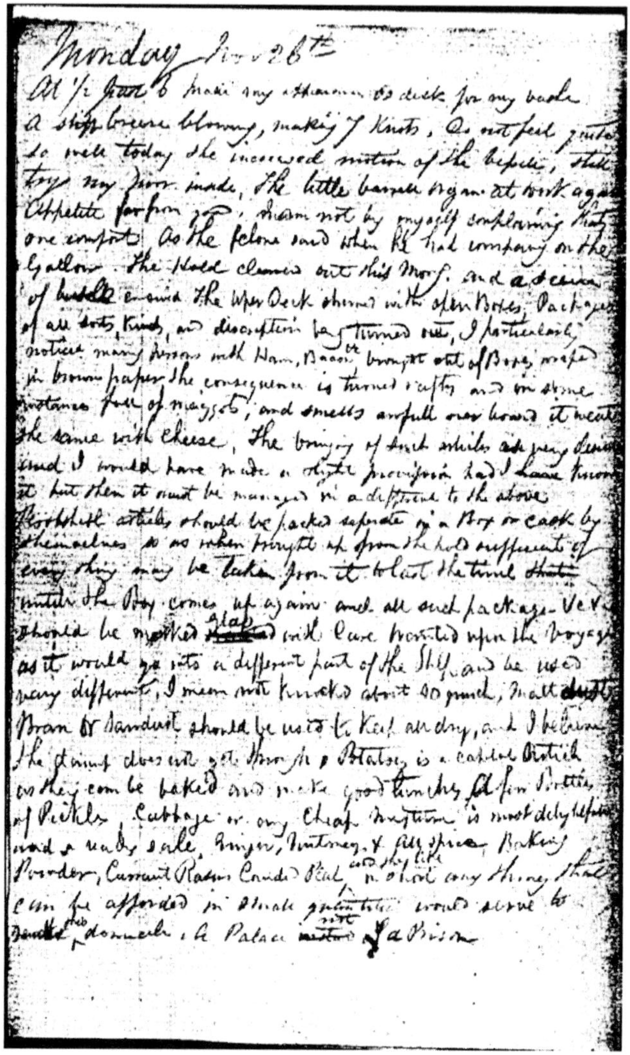
Monday Nov 26th
At 1/2 past 6 make my appearance on deck for my bath
a stiff breeze blowing, making 7 Knots, do not feel quite
so well today the increased motion of the vessel, still
keep my food inside, the little barrel organ at work again
Appetite far from good, I am not by myself complaining that's
one comfort As the felon said when he had company on the
Gallows. The Hold cleaned out this Morng. and a scene
of bustle ensued the Upper Deck strewed with open Boxes, Packages
of all sorts, Kinds, and description being turned out, I particularly
noticed many persons with Ham, Bacon &c brought out of Boxes wrapped
in brown paper the consequence is turned rusty and in some
instances full of maggots, and smells awfull over board it went
the same with Cheese, The bringing of such articles are very desirable
and I would have made a slight provision had I have known
it but then it must be managed in a different to the above
Bottled articles should be packed separate in a Box or cask by
themselves so as when brought up from the hold sufficient of
every thing may be taken from it to last the time that
untill the Box comes up again and all such packages &c
should be marked with care Wanted upon the Voyage
as it would go into a different part of the Ship and be used
very differently, I mean not knocked about so much, Malt dust
Bran or Sawdust should be used to keep all dry, and I believe
the steam does not get through, Potatoes is a capital article
as they can be baked and make good lunches, all fine Bottles
of Pickles, Cabbage or any Cheap Mixture is most delightful
and a ready sale, Ginger, Nutmegs & All spice, Baking
Powder, Currants Raisins Candied Peal and the like in short any thing that
can be afforded in small quantities would serve to
make domestic a Palace not of a Prison

A page from the Diary

THE DIARY

TRANSCRIPT OF PART OF A JOURNAL WRITTEN BY JAMES BROOM WHO SAILED FOR AUSTRALIA FROM PLYMOUTH ABOARD THE *ASIA* IN OCTOBER 1849

Sunday Oct 14th/49

Left Bath by the ½ past 1 o'clock train for Exeter and as beautiful a day as October ever favoured us with. Nature appeared cheerful and gay and helped immediately to dispel from my mind the gloomy thoughts that would intrude themselves in spite of every exertion of mine.

We glided quietly on to Bristol where we had a quarter of an hour to wait. I alighted to procure for myself and a lady in the same carriage some refreshments and afterwards entered into conversation with a young man who was hurriedly pacing the platform exercising himself after being penned up from London. A short conversation with my new acquaintance told me he was upon the same errand as myself, that he had been married only a few days and was going to Plymouth to join his ship. Returning to the carriage was introduced with little ceremony to his wife, Mrs Fountain, who seemed a pleasant and agreeable little woman.

A long and tedious ride brought us to Exeter which we did not reach until dark. We enquired of a passenger the best House for a night's accommodation. They directed us to one at a little distance from the railway, if I remember right the Spotted or Black Cow. We found everything quite to our satisfaction. Refreshing ourselves with tea we took a walk into Exeter. The inhabitants were leaving the different places of Worship and the principal streets thronged. High St appeared to be the principal for Business with many good houses in it, the lower part upon a steep descent. We returned about 9, partook of a little bread and cheese and at ½ past 10 retired to Bed, ordering an early call and breakfast to take the train at 8 the next morning.

Monday October 15th

Awoke in good time. Made my appearance ready for breakfast at 6am. Took an hours walk. Morning cold and frosty. Mr & Mrs F down at 7. Made a hearty breakfast. Left for Plymouth, arrived at half past eleven and proceeded to Mr Willowby's White Horse Hotel Westwell st. Mr F being recommended there by a friend in London. My non acquaintance with the Town and from the appearance of the house I thought I could not do better than remain with them. After seeing to the luggage being made allright we left to find an Eating house much wanting a Dinner. This was soon done and we partook of a little goose. Here we remained resting ourselves very comfortable for a couple of hours. Knowing that it was Mr Brodribb's intention to come down this day I recommended proceeding in the direction of the railway station a chance being that we may see them. As luck would have it we met Mr B and Charles coming into the Town. We took them to our House. Tea was ordered of which we all partook. Discussed over the affairs of Warminster &c. We afterwards walked to the Quay, stroled about until 9 oclock, made the best of our way back and at 11 sought introduction to the chamber.

Tuesday October 16th

Our dejourn a la poulette concluded, we proceeded to the Quay expecting to hear some tidings of the *Asia*. That piece of good luck was however denied us. We then bent our way towards Devonport intending to inspect the Dock Yard, arriving there a little after 11am. The Officer was gone round with another party. We were compeled to defer our visit until 2 oclock. Partook of a lunch Ginger Beer and Bun and walked to the river side to that part called Mutton Cove. There engaged a boat to take us to her Majesties Ship the *Edgincourt*, lookd her all over and found all on board in the most perfect order. Remarked the cleanliness. The Crew were having their dinner and one of them enquired of me if we were come to see the Lions fed. The Sick ward contained only 2 patients. Remained about an hour and then made an hasty return to the Docks. At the entrance gate we waited full an half hour before we could be shown round, during which time the men returned to their work and these appeared to me more employed than at Portsmouth, which Dock I consider better worth looking over than Devonport. Afterwards returned to our Dining Room and again made free with a little Goose. Poultry of every description is remarkable cheap here particularly Geese. Fish we noticed at very low prices and which accounted for our having a fine dish put upon the table every morning for Breakfast. While at Plymouth my appetite (perhaps strange to say) was good all the week This evening call'd upon Mr Harper Junr. Found his shop the largest, and most tastefully fitted up of any in that line in Plymouth. Stroled about for an hour and at an early hour retired to rest.

Wednesday Oct 17th

This morning rather overslep ourselves. Did not make our appearance at the Breakfast Table before 9 oclock. We then sat down to a first rate spread, everything on the Table that could be wished for, and at the moderate charge of only fifteen pence per head. We then walked to the Quay, at least to have a little information respecting our vessel. Not having any we stroled to the Citadel, inspected it and the thought occured to me that Admiral Napier would have his work well cut out to take it, as I believe he has said he could do in half an hour. The Soldiers were exercising. At 1 stroled off for dinner, walked about the remainder of the Afternoon, partook of Tea at the White Horse and spent the Evening at the South Devon Hotel. Heard some good songs, ventriloquism etc. etc. Had the company of Fountain and the Doctor who are very good friends being Doctor to the Ship they are going in. A plentiful supply of punch made that worthy Gentleman exceeding noisy and I thought an early return to the Black Horse desirable. To bed at 12am.

Thursday Oct 18th

Again another fruitless walk to the Quay. Afterwards to the Post Office. Myself and Mr. Brodribb walked round the Market. The Market days are Thursday and Saturday. The show of meat vegetables etc not so good as that appearance of cleanliness as the Bath Market. The Poultry about the same, clean and well laid out. A full supply of Butter Eggs etc and the stalls were nearly all attended by young single women. Several of them were exceedingly good looking plump rosy cheekd farmers daughters. Made a few enquiries of them as to prices, turned a goose or two over and thus passed away another hour. There were also several Drapery Stalls there and Second Hand Clothes, Crockery ware etc with other ill-looking spreads, entirely spoiling the neatness and respectable appearance of the Market. Otherwise it would have been as good as any I have seen out of Bath and London. Returned to the White Horse, refreshed ourselves with a little ale and made preparation for Mr Brodribb' s return to Warminster. We moved off with Carpet Bag, Coats etc at ½ past Eleven, the train starting at 1 pm. There in good time, sauntered about and had an opportunity of seeing the working of the Electric Telegraph, the fourth Devon line having a communication as far as Exeter. Taking leave of Mr B we returned to Dinner. Afterwards to the Hole [Hoe] to see the inspection of the soldier station at the Citadel. It was an inspection day and they went through a number of field movements. Out but little, this Evening being damp and unpleasant. Retired to Bed early, all being heartily tired of stroling about doing nothing but wear out shoe leather and getting rid of our money. Settled my Ac[coun]t with Mrs Willowby as did also Mr Brodribb for his Son.

Friday Oct 19th

This morning breakfasted at our usual hour and immediately proceeded to the Quay, and from the number of walks I have already taken to that part of Plymouth I believe I should experience no difficulty finding my way there blindfolded. Again no tidings and we are beginning to think (the Watermen having told us it has been a fair wind to bring her up for some days) that more than foul wind must be detaining her. Walked towards the Citadel. Met West and wife from Warminster near the Emigration Depot. They walked up with us to the Citadel, listened to the Band playing and stroled about, amusing ourselves in the best possible manner we were able. Obtained the loan of a telescope from a Gentleman through which we had some exceeding good views. The clock stricking one reminded us of our dinner and we stroled off to the eating House. Having heard that the Band would play during the afternoon in the Barrack Yard Devonport I proposed our going there. A Farmer who [was] lodging at the Eating House wished also [to] accompany us. Dinner concluded we bent our steps that way. Was highly pleased with the music and did not begrudge our walk. Returned about 3 pm. Found Mast'r Charles amusing himself writing in his bedroom and Geo Carpenter (A young man going out in the same ship with us also to Adelaide) writing in the Coffee room. I had not been in the house long before Mrs Willowby put into my hands a letter Directed to Mr. Chas. Brodribb and as I was going upstairs asked me to give it to him. I did so and on his opening it found its contents was the anouncement of the arrival of our Ship, purpoting to come from the Agent Mr Wilcox and requiring our attention immediate1y. I returned downstairs to communicate the joyful intelligence and it was soon agreed that we should go there. Off the whole of us marched. I was the first to enter the office and made the enquiry of the clerk who very innocently told me that the ship had not been heard of. I asked him if a letter had not been sent us from their office which he denied. No other proof was required to convince me that a hoax had been practiced on myself and Charley and Master Carpenter now for the first time betrayed himself by laughing most heartily at us, having himself concocted the whole affair. Continued our walk for some time and returned to tea.

Saturday Oct 20th

Information this morning bearing somewhat more the imprint of truth than that of yesterday came to hand and we were told upon authority we had no grounds to question that our long looked for vessel had arrived during the night. This intelligence we hastened to have confirmed and after Breakfast started for Barbican, found all correct, that she came in at 10 the previous night and would sail

Monday or Tuesday. We consulted some time whether we should go on Board this day or not. It was at last agreed that we should visit her with a view only to assertain what would be wanted on the voyage and to look her over. Mr and Mrs Fountain proposed to accompany us. We engaged a Waterman to take us off at 1/6 per hour. During the trip I was very sick. The sea was unusually high although inside the breakwater. This rather confirmed my suspicion as to the illness I was to expect when I started in the ship. We returned after an absence of 2 Hours determining not to go on board again until Monday. At 2 pm dined. Proceeded afterwards to make a few purchases, 3lbs of saltwater soap, Tin Can capable of holding 2 gallons, a few common Towels, ½ dozen col'd [coloured? collared?]shirts 2 pr Bro Cotton Drawers and Common Pair of Wh[ite] Duck Trousers, after which returned to our lodgings to tea at an early hour much better satisfied with the day amusement than any of the preceeding.

Sunday Oct 21st

After playing the lazy life of a Gentleman for now a week we thought it would be as well to sustain the character to our last Day in England, so finished up by having our Sunday morning breakfast in Bed. Arose about eleven, took short strole before dinner. Afternoon, all of us for long walk. Took tea together once more for the last time. Mr & Mrs Fountain and myself to the Independent Chapel. A good and instructive sermon was delivered but the singing far from being what I should have expected from so large a congregation and a chapel at Plymouth. The Building was not the same denomination or quite so large as that of Warminster but of similar formation. No Organ or musical instrument of any kind and I was rather afraid at one time the singing would have come to a stand still. On our return partook of a little of Mrs F's cake, myself providing some brandy and water. Early retiring to once more enjoy the comfort of a good feather Bed perhaps for the last time, if not for the last certainly what we shall not get for the next four or five months.

Monday Oct 22nd

A sojourn at Plymouth a whole week and doing worse than nothing, might well nigh be thought sufficient to satisfy the idle disposition of any one. The past week has really seemed longer than many a month spent in the quiet little town of Warminster. Breakfasted at our normal hour and then moved off to the Quay to make arrangement with some waterman to fetch our Boxes and convey the same with ourselves to the Ship. This completed comfortably reached the vessle by 12 oclock. The Ships dinner contrasted sadly to what I had been lately having. I employed myself principally in getting my Box to the Cabin, packing the Bed in with articles of different kinds for use during the voyage. All was in the utmost state of noisy confusion, going and coming, hauling and swearing. Night closing on us, and having had enough of pacing the decks, about 9 pm retired to try the comfort of a bunk.

Tuesday Oct 23rd

Taking into consideration the change of sleeping appartment, the Bed, the atmosphere, the assault of cockroaches, with noise and drunkeness, I slept tolerably well. This morning the men were engaged taken in water. It was brought in large Barrels and from thence by means of a power Pump passes into the Ship. The decks now begining to be a little clearer and at the close of Evening nearly everything was stowed away into the holds, it being the intention if possible to sail tomorrow.

Wednesday Oct 24th

Preparing this morning for Sailing, the wind however not blowing our direct course, but by tacking we were enabled to make the channel. The Pilot with Captain and Mr Hall came on board about 12 oclock and at 1 pm we were under weigh. We had proceeded but very little distance out of the Breakwater before my anticipations were realised. Goodbye to my dinner of mutton soup and, I was very much afraid, to my inside at the same price. As long as I was able to chew a little biscuit I did so but in less than an hour I was too ill even to keep even to that amusement; in truth I had lost strength to bite it. Remained on deck until the evening when I crawled below, took no inclination for aught save bunk. My first day's sail, a day I shall never forget while memory holds its seat.

Thursday Oct 25th

Did manage to raise myself upright and, after a full quarter of an hours exertion, patience and perseverance, dressed and crawled upon Deck, sat down or rather fell into the first vacant place I saw. I remained about an hour and a half and was absolutely too ill then to prolong my stay any longer. Made for my bed again having left it bad only to return worse. On regaining my cabin I had hardly strength left to pull off my clothes. In truth I did not wait to get it all off but crawled up to my Bunk and was then a little easier. To attempt a description of sea sickness, the different sensations, the weakness and the peculiar effect upon the whole frame, would impose a task far beyond my limited powers of explication. A few words must suffice. Those who have drank too much, enough to be in a decided case of inebriation, upon laying themselves down found the Bed, the room and all things in it going round and round and obliged to hold by it to keep themselves in it, head aching violently, at the same time sick, not able to keep even a little tea upon their stomachs, can form the best idea of sea sickness. Before I came on board the *Asia* I knew nothing of illness. I can no longer boast of that. Two or three days of it is quite difficult for any one. Had it have lasted much longer I should undoubtedly wishes myself back again at Warminster or indeed anywhere else upon terra ferma. What seemed to make it so much the worse I could not obtain any thing that I could fancy. Scarcely any one came to see me and all I could get was a little tea. Nothing could I eat for 2 days. Sleep came to my relief and thus closed the fourth day on board the *Asia*.

Friday Oct 26th

The experience of yesterday taught me it was much easier with my head on my Pillow. I could not therefore persuade myself to keep up longer than an hour. My spirits were not quite so bad as yesterday and it was remarked by some that I should soon be up and all right again. Mr White, a young man (last situation in Buckingham palace) in the cabin as myself, has been obliged to keep his Bed ever since they left London now nearly a month.

Treated myself with Bottle of Port Wine for which I paid 2/6. Not very first rate quality but better than nothing and I drank about half the first day. Felt myself much improved.

Saturday Oct 27th

This morning arose at the same hour as the rest. Partook of a little dinner which settled tolerably well. Ship rolling about in fine style upsetting everything that was not actually nailed but not forgetting ourselves. Even when holding with both hands had the greatest difficulty to keep upon a seat. Placed myself early between the sheets but alas not to sleep but to amuse myself with kicking and knocking off the cockroaches. These tormenting creatures are of quite a different species to what I ever saw before, about 3 times as large as those seen in England, of a dark Brown color with long wings, fly and with an innumerable quantity of legs. I have been told they are peculiar to India and came over in old Casks, ship sides, lumber etc. They give a sharp stinging bite and what with that and crawling it is a long time before I can get to sleep.

Sunday Oct 28th

After Breakfast part of the church service was read but no sermon. There was only a few in attendance. It was read by one of the midshipmen. To bed early but far from feeling well. Should have liked a little gruel, sago, Arrow Root anything of the like. These articles should always be taken on a voyage, because altho not much of each may be required yet if a little when wanted. It is looked upon just at the time as a luxury and one then feels ample repayed for the little trouble and outlay attending the collection of these trifling little articles.

Monday Oct 29th

Awoke this morning at my usual time ½ past Seven feeling thankful for a decided improvement both in health and spirits, but not with that disposition, or rather capability, to make myself generally usefull a feeling absolutely necessary to carry out the duties of Captain of the Mess to the satisfaction of all. Dinner today consisted of boiled Pork (as it is called) or rather thick piece of a fat pig in pickle, great lumps of fat 6-8 inches thick and with neither the taste of Pork or Bacon. Shortly after dinner a Steam Boat hoved into sight, signalling as distressed. Orders were immediately given to lower the Two side Boats. It was done with great dispatch, as near as I could guess the time not exceeding 5 or 10 minutes, they were both alongside manned and waiting orders to pull off. As soon as the vessel came sufficiently near they were dispatched with instructions that our Captain was willing to render all the assistance necessary or what otherwise may be required. She proved to be the *Pandora* steamer made expressly for service on the Indian Rivers and made originally to the order of The Pasha of India, but he being dethroned before its completion it remained in the hands of the builders and by them sent out on speculation of finding a Customer. It was one of the most beautiful little vessels, of 150 Tons burden with Engines of 90 Horse Power, belonged to Robinson & Co, bound to Cairo. In shape and ornamental work it did not appear of English manufacture. Massive Gilt figure Head and profusion of Copper Ornaments upon her Bows with a great quantity of gilt moulding around the raised part of her deck which was in part of the Engine. Some idea may be formed of the beauty and essence attending her building when the fact is known that insurance of 1400£ was effected upon her, 500£ being paid for the same being insured as double hazardous. This was information from one of the crew and therefore may not be correct in every particular. Her captain was a sad contrast to our own, a tall, ugly, overgrown, ill proportioned man, about 45 years of age, eyes particularly large and ugly head. All on board our ship was excitement bustle, particularly at the time when it was thought she would go down, 2 of our midshipmen being on board her during the time hands were at work getting away the moveables. 2 hours served to strip her. She was spoken with at ½ past one and at ¼ past 3 for the first time in my life I witnessed the turn up of a vessel.

All on board the *Asia* seemed pleased and thankful that they had been the happy means of saving 12 fellow creatures who gratefully acknowledged it. We lost by the detention about 20 miles.

Tuesday Oct 30th

Cold wind and much rain. Strong case of the disagreeable. Appetite not good, or rather, I should say, not good enough to do with Tea and Biscuit. Something wanted of a more tempting description. At ten eat a little of the ginger Bread laid in when at Plymouth. Made pudding to be eat with the Pork. It turned out to the general satisfaction of our Mess. Consider it was my first attempt at Pudding making did not consider it so very bad. Afternoon had head ache. Towards the close of the day a strong breese sprang up, the sea running mountains high and ship rolling fearfully. I attributed my been so queer to the motion as I could not get on at tea time, and was obliged to depart early to Bunk. No vessel in sight this day or any thing occured requiring notice.

Wednesday Oct 31st

Dressed and washed myself this morning within a few minutes of my usual time not having slept a wink after 3 oclock. The night cold and very boisterous. Ship rocked tremendous. The water during the night came in and some of my things were floating. My unfortunate G[rea]t Coat, which I placed upon the Bed when I got into it with the hope being warmed, tumbled upon the floor and was saturated with water and very dirty. If a landsman at this time could have looked into our cabin he would have had an opportunity of forming some idea of the comforts of a voyage to sea. I have before told you that one of the inmates of my Cabin was a Mr White. He left a good situation in Buckingham Palace on ac[coun]t of his health not being very good, and seeks a restoration by a sea voyage. Unless finer weather and the appartment is cleaner he will only be laying the foundation of consumption. Improving his present health is quite out of the question. On deck nearly all the morning, wind cold and boisterous. At 11 partook of a little cake of home manufactory and quite a treat. I enjoyed it better than any thing I have eat since on board. I may here mention a few things that would have added much to the comfort of a voyage. It is not a quantity of clothes as many lay in, because one has neither the opportunity or inclination to wear them. Any old common things do for sea use as long as they are decent and becoming, but something in the way of eatables, as it often seems the appetite is not good and we cannot fancy the ships provisions. A few bread loaves, cut into slices and again baked and keep dry, is an excellent substitute for the biscuits for lunch, or in case a dinner of pork cannot be got on with, bread and cheese will be realished. An onion would also assist to [-] it down. A small quantity of well dryd Beacon lay in as a slice for Breakfast, when perhaps it may be, as it has often been my case, there is nothing but biscuits and Tea or Coffee for the meal. A few Bottles of Pickles or a large Jar of Pickled Cabbage will be found all there. To bed early.

Thursday Nov 1st

The night and morning cold and Boisterous. No sleep after 5 am. Turned out at the usual hour. Some cold boiled rice left from yesterday dinner formed my breakfast. At 11 took lunch, Biscuit, cheese and a Pickled Onion. Dinner Cold Pork and suet Pudding. The vessel rolling from side to side obliged me to hold on with one hand and use the other to get our meal. To prevent the things from rolling off the table strained across a rope and so put the articles things between them. The dinner time was one scene of confusion noise and laughter, soup plates and panicans flying in all directions. This morning turned out Boxes and found the water and damp had much affected the articles near the bottom. I should here name that Boxes brought to sea cannot well be too strong. Strips of board nail'd across the bottom to raise them from the deck and allow a current of air to pass underneath is indispensable. The want of this precaution may cause great disappointment. Had I not have this early looked to my Box I doubt not every pot of Jam with Cake etc would have been spoiled. This afternoon sighted Two Ships one homeward the other outward bound, the former 4 the latter about 7 miles distant. With a continuance of fair wind may expect to reach Madeira by Sunday morning. I am, with many others, looking forward to our getting there with pleasure, hoping to have warmer and dryer weather. This now wet and cold, at intervals blowing very hard. Few can keep their footing on deck. Our sick list is rather lessening from what I can learn. There is about 12 under the doctors hands. At an early hour retired to Bed, but not to sleep, for at about 11 oclock a dreadfull row was commenced. Nothing would be heard but swearing, noise and confusion, talking of fighting with the worst of language. We have on board 4 or 5 of the desperate bad characters who seem only pleased when they are quarelling or exciting other to it.

Squalls, heavy sea, ship rolling violently.

Friday Nov 2nd

A continuance of bad weather. Wind high and very cold, blowing nearly a gale, sea running mountain high. Have been going during the last 12 hours at the rate of 8 knots, the greater speed yet made. At 12 midday was passed by a small French Merchant vessel homeward bound to St. Malo. Had some conversation with the crew of the *Pandora* and from them learned their opinion of our vessel. They considered her exceedingly strong built and although the sea was breaking over continually and tossing her about violently there was not heard a creaking of her timbers. She is built entirely of teak, considered the hardest and strongest wood that grows. Not a vessel made for show but service and durability.

Dined this day from Pickled Salmon. Not bad eating and well desirable for a change. The arrangements of our ship with regard to serving out the different stores is as follows. At 7 oclock am Biscuit. At ¼ past 2pm Grog. 4 water daily. On Saturday mornings, Flour raisins suit sugar mustard and vinegar. Flour and suit also on Tuesday and Thursday with Pork, Beef, Soup, Bouilli, Preserved Mutton and beef with Potatoes at no stated times, convenience being the rule.

Saturday Nov 3rd

Very wet, cold and squally Morning. Arose about 7 oclock For Breakfast Pickled salmon. Dinner today Pork and Pea Soup. The Captain today not very well. Am told he is obliged to take Medicine every night suffering from costiveness [constipation]. His mode of living is very different to ours. They get in the Cuddy a good spread at every meal, wine spirits and fruit on the table after dinner, Fowls and Duck killed twice week The duck are in tolerable good condition but the fowls are only fit for a curry and are generally dressed for breakfast. This Evening we had our first Concert or Harmonic Meeting and to those who had never witnessed such a scene on board a ship before would have look'd on with considerable interest. Every part of the lower deck from middle to fore Hatch was litteraly cramed with Ladies, Gentlemen and at the back could be seen several of the sailors. The Songs as may be supposed were of a very varied character, good bad and indifferent. Two from my list helped to swell the list of bad ones, after which they contrived to entirely demolish the form we sat upon, not a part left even sufficient to sit upon during meals.

2pm furious squalls with a mountainous sea. Close reefed the fore topsail and treble reefed Main topsail. Carpenter seeing hatches. Heavy seas broke over us.

Sunday Nov 4th

Rolled about in prime style all night. Arose rather earlier than usual, having Plum Duff to make for Dinner. Altho this is my first attempt it will no doubt give perfect satisfaction as our appetites are such as need but little tempting. The sea air has doubtlessly considerable improved all and few now appear very particular as to what it is, quantity being the principal desirability. Our cabin which had been in a very wet and dirty state for several days was shown to the Captain who ordered our servant to give it another cleaning. We all set to work and baled out 2 or 3 buckets of water. I then turned in and had a good night. Moon fine.

Monday Nov 5th

A considerable change for the best this morning, the decks presenting a different appearance being dry and that is more than I can say for any day since our departure. They are now clean and comfortable as also our Cabin. The air compared to what we have had it is soft and balmy. Although we are not proceeding on our journey so rapidly the wind having abated yet the hours do not seem so long and wearysome. I should say with the little knowledge I have of the matter, every stick of sail being set we are doing 6 knots per hour. Hope to sight Madeira at Middle day tomorrow. The anchor is being made ready and we are in hopes of at least getting a few hours there. The warmth and fineness of the afternoon seams to liven all. A goodly number making their appearance upon the poop reminding me of a gipsy party sitting upon the deck in small parties in full conversation. A motley group, there not being to my taste a pretty girl amongst them. Charles and myself walked together this evening, and discussed the probably doings at Warminster, Bonfire and Fireworks being the order of the Evenings amusement we strongly suspected. We did all we could towards keeping up the day. Dressed up a man as guy faulks and carrying him round the ship. This created a good laugh and helped to pass away an hour. Turn'd into bed early.

Sighted P[orto] Santo

Tuesday Nov 6th

Disturbed a couple of hours before my usual time by noise and confusion extending from one end of the vessel to the other. The Cry of land and get up you are loosing a splendid view was echoed from one end of the ship to the other. I hastily obeyed the summons turning out at 5 am. After Breakfast took sketch for you. We have now but little wind and not making more than 2 knots per hour and standing 2 miles from shore opposite the little Island of Porto Santo. The weather has assumed a more settled aspect reminding one of a beautiful summers day in England. It is said we are 15 miles from Madeira. Had hope to be there by dinner time 1 or 2 oclock. 5 am we are at last hoved in sight of the principal town of Madeira, Funchall. To the left of us stands the Island known as the deserted Island, no use being made of it. The mass of high Black Rocks little or no vegetation appearing. This Town contains 1800 Inhabitants 2 thirds of the whole Island. At the distance we are from the shore it has the appearance of a confused jumble of little White Houses with no order or pretention to architectural beauty. After coming within ½ mile of the place a Boat came off to us bringing the Dock and Harbour Master 2 assistants and 4 sailors. He spoke English well but with a foreign accent. His enquiries were respecting any ship and country, the time we left England, etc. etc. also of the *Pandora* Captain, and to our surprise and disappointment to many informed us that not a man of our crew could come ashore without our first standing Quarantine 5 days. But the crew of the *Pandora* should however be taken off the following morning to the Lazerette About 8 or 9 oclock and he would bring us off bread and fruit. I noticed a novel made of using their oars. Instead of these being loose, that is working at the side of their Boats, between two pegs or little uprights, they had a broad flat piece of board nearly circular about a foot from the end of the oar in the centre of which was a hole and rocked upon a peg, instead of as we do between them. The flat piece of wood was about the size of a small pudding plate. They used them with equal dexterity rowing quite as fast as our watermen could have done. Their Boats also are flat Bottom clumsy and larger than those used upon the Thames with a high prow or figure head. As soon as this functionary had taken his leave our captain ordered all hands to the shipabout intending to stand out to sea and come in again in the morning. A brisk breeze had sprang up during the last 2 or 3 hours and I think to look upon that as the softest movement. I am now sitting writing this at 7 pm and if I did not know that I was in a ship could not tell it from the motion. Not quite so much noise today. The noisy ones being smokers are regaling them with a little Cavendish upon deck, no smoking or open light of any kind allowed between decks. The Lazerette with them is the same as an Hospital to us, and is situated as far as I could judge from the ship about 2 miles from the town. The sailors and Captain both will have to be there 5 days in quarantine.

[Loose page at one time pinned between November 6th and 7th]

Santo, an island in the Atlantic Ocean 300 miles of the coast of Africa and one of those call'd the Madeiras. It is about 15 miles in circumference and produces but little corn. There [?] and wild hogs and a vast number of rabbits, trees which produce gum or resin called dragon's blood, and likewise a little good honey and wax. It has no harbour; but good anchorage in the roads. It belongs to the Portuguese and is in Lon 16.20 W Lat. 32.58 N

Madeira. This Island is in the form of a triangle. It is said to have been discovered by an English Gentleman in - 44 and conquered by the Portuguese in 1431. But the most remarkable fact spoken of is their setting fire to a forest with a design to warm themselves which continued burning for several years and the ashes rendered the soil extremely fertile especially in wine which it produces in great quantities and keeps best in the hottest climate in the torrid zone. [End of entry]

Wednesday Nov 7th

The early part of this Morning was cold with two or 3 heavy showers which obliged us to quit for a short time the deck. I turned out about 6 am in the hope of getting a Salt water Bathe in the fore deck and promenade before Breakfast but disappointed. When the sun is not over cast it is beautiful. The air is soft and exhilarating. The breeze is not so hot as I expected we should have it when at Madeira, knowing how beautiful the grape ripen there. I name this, not that I forget that their Summer is past and we are enjoying the cool part of their year, but I had so long looked forward to our reaching this far on our voyage that I am rather disappointed it is not hotter. After breakfast which consisted of Chocolate and a little cake (not yet being able to make a meal of Biscuits) the Portuguese boats came along side at the appointed hour to take off the men, or I should rather have said to bring us fruit and one of them to show the way to the Lazerette. Two of our Boats carried the men and their Luggage and which detained us about 3 hours. We were none of us sorry being obliged to wait as it gave us the opportunity to have another boat of fruit. The supply consisted of Bread loaves, Apples, oranges, wall nuts (grown in England and good for nothing) Bananas (the nearest thing that I can compare this fruit to as regards taste is an English Fig but sweeter. There being no acid with it it is rather incipid) and a few onions. The Captain gave 5£ for the lot, including 10/- for the mens trouble, and thought to be worth upon the island not more 2£. 1 oclock pm under all sail and proceeding pleasantly on our voyage. After Dinner (The best pea soup Pork and Potatoes we have yet had) a rather animated scene took place upon the Poop. It was the division of the Fruits. All was arranged out in 15 or 16 lots amounting to 6/8 [6s 8d] each mess and given to the respective Captain to be by them again divided. This division was soon made and so the fun followed. The little loaves about the size of a good penny one at home were sold at 6d, oranges fetched 4 pence each with ready bargain and it was said would sell at 2/6 each under the line and their jackets at 1/- more. Walnuts at a discount. Bananas quick sale at 2d each and for an hour after all was fun, speculation and noise. Spoke with merchant vessel *The Tropic* bound for Serealone [Sierra Leone]. She remained in sight the whole afternoon. Made this day 100 miles. Tired and glad to get to bed at 9 oclock.

Thursday Nov 8th

Beautiful morning indeed and the sun shining most delightfull. We are proceeding about 7 knots, with almost an unruffled sea and cloudless sky with little or no motion to the ship. Nothing occurred this morning to afford me a subject for comment. Everything is progressing steadily and with comfort to all and I may venture to express a hope we have now got over the worse of everything. We have still 2 or 3 on the invalide list, one a young man in consumption and another a lady in a delicate state of health and some think is not going to be well during the voyage. She has no spirit to do the least thing, is as helpless as a child. It is a young married lady, married about 10 days before we started, and her Husband is most attentive waiting upon her. There is nothing that she can like that the ship can afford but what she has, yet she does not get strong. On the contrary it is thought by many she is declining fast. Suet Pudding and peas and mutton for dinner.

Friday November 9th

Wind rather higher today and did not find it quite so warm, still very pleasant on board and for the mornings amusement I did a little sketching. I have had a Book of instruction lent me which I shall practise a little thinking I shall find much amusement from it. After Dinner of pork and salmon (the latter we put away for breakfast) I walked upon the fore castle to watch the process of washing amongst the sailors. It is not practised by the Passengers and indeed were they desirous of doing so it would be the same, little or nothing would be done on that part of the ship amongst the sailors. There is no washing tubs. Every large article such as trousers or jacket [laid?] upon the deck and rub'd with a brush. I had given a Towel and 1 pr of stockings just to see the effect of their washing. Cold salt water and soap used induces one to think I shall have them back a beautiful color. Every thing passed off the remainder of the day much the same as usual. This evening had conversation with two of the Passengers who are Drapers and bound to the same place as myself. They hope not to be obliged to follow the old Trade. They dislike it much and will not, unless compelled by finding nothing else to do. One Gentleman has part of a Drapery Stock with him. He is likewise bound to Adelaide, an Independent and one of those little quiet men peculiar to the cloth. Not been married very long. Has his wife with him some few years his junior. Made this day 117 miles.

Saturday Nov 10th

How very different is the state of the weather we are now passing through to what under any ordinary circumstance may be expected in England. Instead of the unpleasant mists cold dripping rain and bleak winds, we have exactly that temperature with an unclouded sky known about July or August. We expect as we near the Equator to have it much warmer. We however shall not be very much puzzled what to be at then. A top coat cast off and thin blouse or other light covering substituted will have the desired effect. The sea breeze cools and softens the atmosphere so that the heat is not felt as on shore. I am told that there may be a chance of my having to complain of the heat by and by but I doubt it much. When a person has been leading for years a comparatively idle life, a sort of Gentleman life, that on board a ship would doubtlessly please much. I am sure never when a Boy at school did I look forward with more pleasure to the arrival of Holliday time than I do to that day I shall again set foot on terra ferma at Port of Adelaide. Nothing will please me more than again finding myself between a pair of good traces, and easy collar on. It may be that after 4 months idleness (a pretty good apprenticeship) I shall be a little inclined to kick over them, but a good light cash will perhaps have the desired effect to get me to work steadily again At ½ past 7 pm was held for the first time our Concert vocal and musical. Considering it was the first appearance of many and before quite a large audience a few songs were sung in the desired style. We have 3 or 4 tolerable vocalists amongst us. Our endeavours seem to give generall satisfaction. After promising better things for the future the meeting separated at 9 oclock highly approving of the Evenings entertainment. I will at some future period give a programme but time will not this day permit. Another week terminated and leaving us, with only 2 exceptions, all in good health, which for my part I endeavour to feel truly thankful for.

Mr Box dismissed as acting 3rd Officer for neglect of duty while the water was being served out in the fore hold. Instead of doing his duty Mr B went into the cabin of Mrs Francis.

Sunday Nov 11th

Making our Plum Puddings and preparing Dinner before 8 am permitted my being ready to attend divine Service which for the first time was held upon the middle or quarter deck, and to one that had never witnessed the like before it was a very impressive scene. The Union Jack was unfurled over the capsan, and the service read in a very impressive manner by Mr Lakewood, one of the Passengers, a tall, fine man, quite the Gentleman and good reader. The whole was done in a style that would not have disgraced any Pulpit in England. It was a goodly sermon and I enjoyed it much. We commenced by singing the morning Hymn, the Service, through to the Communion, then sang 4 verses of the 92nd Psalm, concluding with a short exhortation from the Epistle of Jude, 20 verse, But ye beloved, building yourselves in your most holy faith, praying in the Holy Ghost. After Dinner (preserved mutton and pudding) I attended at 2 past 3, prayer, between deck for the use of Dissenters. We had Full Service and good Lecture read, from the 12 of Hebrews and part of the 23 verse, to the general assembly. The Captain Doctor and many of the Principal Passengers joined us and I may here add that to much praise cannot be awarded to the Captain for his kind attention, and arrangement to our every comfort, more particularly regarding the enjoyment of the Sabath. The Evening Church Service was held at ½ past seven, saying the 100th and 105th Psalm concluding with the Evening Hymn. The Sermon was the remaining half of that delivered in the morning and from the pen of the Rev'd Mark English of Dublin. It was a pretty sight all standing round uncovered with ten lamps burning over head (those used to light the ship later). The seats were placed to form a square the width of vessel. The night very dark which added much to the solemnity of the occasion presented. It reminded me of some Foreign picture I had formerly seen, such as a Hudson Point by torch light or something quite of Foreign appearance.

How good and pleasant must it be
To thank the Lord most high
And with repeated hymns of praise
His name to magnify.

I retired for the night at 9 oclock thankful for the opportunity of spending another earthly Sabath in the manner I had, it being considerably more to my satisfaction than the last.

Monday Nov 12th

All is quietness, order and every comfort, moving on but slowly, nearly becalmed. At mid day not doing more than 2 knots perhaps. The weather at last is such as requires a little alteration in my wearing apparel, something not quite as heavy as cloth would be exceptable. I am thinking of making my little coat come in useful again, I suppose for the last time of asking. I mean the one you gave me some four year back and the one that clients so much admired at Warminster at different times, so that is the one I allude to. It is pretty well known there I know. I may as well here remark, that I would recommend all who have not a thin Tweed coat to have some light in that way but let it be dark, the darker the better, and the commoner also, provided it be strong. It is no use to have light, washing things on board. A pair of white Drills or Duck Trousers is not more than 2 days wear, to look decent. There is so much sitting about and that upon pitchy or varnished spars, that one would be sure to pick it up somewhere or other let him be ever so carefull. The Ships Company engaged this afternoon changing the sails, putting up lighter ones and making the old do in the place of the new that has hitherto been used. Our new sails cost but a short time ago 400£, the Rope and other Tackeling £350 more. This afternoon employed myself reading and the Evening listening to the Piano being played by Mrs Lakewood and the Misses Neald. It has been removed from the lower deck where it stood in a case to the Cuddy Captain's Apartment. It belongs to a Mr Hawke, who with his wife is going to Sydney, that is if she lives long enough to reach there. The first set of Quadrilles were danced as also 1 Country Dance. This brought to a close another Monday Evg.

Tuesday Nov 13th

We have now entered the Tropic of Cansor Latitude 23 Longitude 34. An unruffled sea. Motion of the vessel scarcely perceivable, and not doing more than 2 knots. It is thought we are come about 1000 miles from Madeira. Dancing resumed again this Evening. Did the polite to Mrs Smith, handed her through the first bit of Quadrilles. The ladies rather idle this Eve[nin]g and requiring much pressing, the effect of the hot day I suppose. I readily excuse them although it is now cool enough for anything in the shape of a quiet dancing. Now the Evenings have become so fine and warm many of our young men do not think of turning in for the night before 1 or 2 oclock. Some have begun to sleep upon the table that we eat from. These are the ones that annoy us with their nightly revels and drinking and carousing, few know to what time in the mornings.

Wednesday Nov 14th

A stiff Breeze (compared to what we had yesterday) sprang up towards morning and at 9 am we are making our way through the mighty ocean certainly not fast but very sure and in every way pleasant and desirable. Amused myself this afternoon by playing my violin for an hour or two. The Stores opened also for the sale of eatables, and drinkables, belonging to the Captain. I will name a few of the prices different articles are fetching so that you may see as I have done, the necessity of being provided with such commodities if thought required or would assist to make the voyage more agreeable. Tolerable good cheese weighing 9lbs 10/- each - Bacon 1/4 lb Ham (anything but first rate) 1/6 lb. The cheapest article supplied is wine and Spirit but it may be remember the quality of all except the rum is very inferior. Brandy, Port and Sherry 1/6 bottle, Lime juice 3/- Do, Ginger Beer and Lemonade and Porter 1/- Eggs 6d each. This Evening for the first time received invitation from the Captain to bring my violin upon the Poop to play for dancing. I do so and it was kept up with great spirit until nearly 10 oclock They quite tired me several times, but I hope soon with a little practice to turn the tables and be able to play them down instead of my being the first to cry out. Retired, very much satisfied with my Evenings amusement.

Thursday Nov 15th

Wind, blowing East with strong breeze. Course South ½ West. Speed 6 knots, until 4 pm when we increased to 7 knots.

This morning large quantities of flying fish were seen. They do not come very near the vessel and appear like a little flight of Swallows. 20 or more rise out of the water together and fly or rather skim the surface for 20 or 30 yards. Their flights are said to take place when persued by the Benetas or other fish that pray upon them. They are known also to jump out of the water at a light and Boats thus fitted are used to catch them. They are sold at St Helena in the Market, like mackerel in ours and not unlike them for eating, considered very good but scarce. This eveng spent much like the preceding. The violin in requisition from 8 to 10. Feel rather queerish. Suppose it is the increased motion of the ship, caused by the swell of the sea here. I do not think I shall ever make a good sailor. I suppose I am not fond enough of it. For supper partook of a little neat Brandy and cake hoping to produce a desire for sleep but alas my inside was not to be persuaded to settle matters in this manner. I therefore emptied my cupboard of its entire contents and placed myself, dinner, tea and supperless, down for another night. What affects a nights slumber will have upon matters as they now stand I will tell you in the morning.

Friday Nov 16th

Every stitch of available canvas set and we are skimming over the silvery waves, 8 knots per hour. This vessel being very broad at her bows, short and lying deep in the Water has never been known to do more than 11 knots per hour and that was in a gale off the Cape of Good Hope. The number of Sails this ship could be made to carry is 26, altho that number is never used. Some would be of no service. Those now in use are the Flying Gib, Standing Gib, Fore top mast staysail, Fore Sail, Fore Top Sail, Fore top Gallant Sail, Fore Royal Main Sail, Main. During the afternoon 3 more sails were up. Appetite much improved and I hope to go along all right for some time. I shall take care not to get tipsy. My head is all right now and I have made up my mind to stick to the cold water system. Night fine and clear.

Saturday Nov 17th

This morning passed off quietly and all things moving satisfactory on board I found amusement reading. A vessel discerned early, guessed at the distance of 12 miles, outward bound to the coast of South America or the [Brazils?]. For the first time I opened my Clothes Box. I have not required anything before although I might have had things before as it was not passed into the Hold. Many Boxes that came on board at Plymouth were stowed away in two spare Cabins. I have now taken out 2 Blue Striped Shirts, a couple of Old Flannel Waist [waistcoats] 1 pair of Duck Trowsers 1 Pair of Cotton Drawers to wear with them if required and am determined not to again take any thing more out for wear before I reach Adelaide. I purpose using as little as possible, limiting myself to 1 col'd Shirt and Flannel a week and when dirty wash them myself so as not to have more than 1 shirt require washing on my arrival. Stockings have not been worn some time and will not be again unless driven to by cold weather which is unexpected as well as not wished for. This afternoon made my Plum Duff for tomorrow dinner, wishing if possible to do without being thus engaged upon Sundays. Would that I may always bear in mind not to defer until tomorrow what can be done today. Concert this Evening as usual. All passed as quiet as on previous occasions and conducted in the most praiseworthy manner. Not being very sleepy and so beautiful an Evening I did not retire for the night before eleven oclock. To those who did not know from experience the difference of atmosphere upon deck to that below in the Cabin they would never believe it. It seems almost overpowering and I have paused at the door of mine several times reflecting whether it would be of any use my attempting to sleep there the night. A short time however suffices to get use to it, about 10 minutes, but still the heat cannot be got over. This we counteract by laying with nothing on except a thin flannel. During the day was exhibited and carried about a flaming bill attached to a board announcing that the Celebrated Kissangho from London was engaged at an immense expense and having just arrived would give his wonderful exhibition this Evening and all were invited to "Go and see the wonderfull Kissankoo opened to all, equalled by none". At 8 oclock the Concert commenced by the Band 2 flutes/violin playing select airs. The singers whose names were before made known came forward as call'd by the leader (Colonel Simpson). All went off remarkably well except the manuves of the wizard. The rolling of the ship rather spoild his fun but altogether it was not bad for our present situation and as good as may be expected. Much like the persuit of amusement (not knowledge) under difficulties.

Sunday Nov 18th

I cannot say I enjoyed the service of this day as last Sunday. There was not that solemnity observed or seriousness in the meeting that prevailed on former occasions, from some unexplained cause. The morning prayer as also sermon was very short and hurried over. The Hymn sing to tunes few if any knew. It was rather better in the Evening but I did not enjoy my Sunday as I had looked forward to. I shall therefore pass it over without further remarks hoping, if spared to see another, matter will improve. I was lent a very interesting work on divinity which occupied every spare moments during the day and which sufficiently interested me to prevent my leaving it until read through. Thus closed another Sabath spent anything but to my satisfaction. This I cannot refrain from naming as others expressed the same feeling as myself

Monday Nov 19th

This day scarcely a change from the ordinary routine of daily duties, both of Ships Crew and Passengers. I have before spoken of our Captain being a most obliging, considerative and Gentlemanly Man and there then being but little that occurs today requiring comment I think I cannot do better than refer once more for the last time to that subject. A more convenient opportunity may not at a future period occur. As day by day rolls on I cannot but observe that it matters not in what situation in life we are placed or what part of life's drama we are call'd upon by Providence but that there is an equal amount of watchfulness, perseverence and energy required to sustain it carry out and fill with honour and respectability. Unceasing application and perseverance is also required and we are all induced readily to admit that aparient difficulties however great at first sight, are by the exercise of two such qualifications soon reduced from mountains into mole hills. As we are told, troubles and difficulties met upon the threshold are half conquered. A Man of mercantile Persuits, more particularly, ought to possess the above enumerated good qualities. It should form the principal feature in his character who is entrusted with the lives, comfort and wellbeing of his fellow creatures. I have been thus particular in giving my idea of desireable qualifications for a man of Business, and endeavour to show that I have a slight idea of how things ought to be, it being my intention to close these few remarks by observing that the foregoing allutions are made to our own Captain, as his behaviour towards us would fully justify those abilities which enable him to appear the Gentleman and the sailor.

Tuesday Nov 20th

Slow and sure must be the motto of the *Asia* for at the speed we are going today, little is wanted to induce that belief that we shall be one of the occupiers of this proud traverser of the mighty deep for the space of 4 months, is also becoming pretty well a confirmed fact. This morning I had a chat with three or four of our little Town amusing myself with the observations and different answers received from questions I put, as to what they would like best in the way of eatables and Drinkables could they land at Port Adelaide this morning. Varied indeed were their replys. Some were for a Bottle of wine, another would give anything for a Glass of good clear spring water, a second for Bread and Cheese with an onion. A third would order a jolly good Dinner, a tuck out, and no mistake, while a fourth more moderate wished only to put his mouth to a pint of good Stout. But the last, a man judging his appetite from size of mouth, head and shoulders and sature in general, could eat a Donkey, and a sack of shavings gave me as what he would like best.

Wednesday Nov 21st

Heavy rain at 4 am. Arose this morning feeling rather uneasy, not quite myself, either eat too much yesterday or for the want of it, I could hardly determine which, but no mistake about my being obliged to quit my domicile half an hour before my usual time and make a hasty appearance on deck - quietly seated there perched up as I would have call one, on the babys in the wood, when to the discomforture of my Trousers and Flannel waist, over my head descended a couple of Buckets of Water, a substitute of no mean character for a shower Bathe at sea. Had I have been otherwise attired I should not have cared but the drying of such articles could only be done in the sun and therefore attended with some little inconvenience. The sailors observed me enter the little Box and like them always ready for a lark quietly made for the place, poured the water upon the top and through the [scotches?]. It descended pretty freely. A Dozen of them waited to see me make my egress, when at my expense they enjoyed a good laugh. Obliged to make my appeance in White Duck. It will be for the day only, and while the Cloth and Kersymere is drying. Amongst passing events I do not forget that we have been now more than 1 month in board this craft, one month since we steer'd out of Harbour at Plymouth. Time and Tide truly waits for no man, and situated as I now am I have no particular wish that it should.

Thursday Nov 22nd

All very quiet and going on as comfortable as circumstances will permit. Speed 4 knots. Much rain the early part of this morning cleared up again about 10 am. Sun not so hot, should think in the shade about 80. Determined that the rain should not deprive me of my Bathe so borrowed a large waterproof coat and nothing else on proceeded to the fore Castle. Several others were engaging the same refreshing amusement and I may here tell you how we manage to have what we call our Bathe. We strip and have 6 or 8 Buckets of water poured over our heads which answers the purpose extremely well and from the number of Buckets used we get a thorough wetting all over. After wiping myself as dry as the rain would permit I returned to my cabin to complete my Toilet for the day. This afternoon for the first time did a little washing. A Cotton Pocket Hdkf [Handkerchief] and 2 pr. Cotton Stockings were the articles practised upon. I had some difficulty to get them dried. Obliged to watch them and move them about first to one place and then another, no getting them into the sight. Afterwards turned out Box and found 2 silk Hdkfs spotted and the color nearly gone, everything so damp that I was afraid my pots of Jam and Honey were spoiled but to my greatest satisfaction they appeared all as good as when I left England. Intend not to touch them untill all my cake is gone. I have been obliged to allow myself to a very small slice every Evening for the past week at Supper time, about ½ past nine or 10 with a little [- d] and soda with a dash of Brandy in it. The contents of the Brandy Bottle too, is in the last stage of Consumption. When gone, and I find the water is so bad as not to be drank without something in it, I have 2/6 laid aside to replace it. I sold some of my oranges for that money. I fancied it would answer my purpose than to eat oranges at 4d each. The Rum is served out at ½ past 2 pm and is about a wine glass to each. In our Mess only we take it by turns to have the whole instead of dividing it daily. We find it much more convenient as I drink but little myself not liking it and I have some always ready to give away for any little thing done for me. Twice I have been obliged to have the loan of the Carpenters glue Pot for my Violin, which threatens to come to pieces. What with damp from the floor and heat from where my violin is kept (in my bunk) I am quite at a loss to know what to be at with it. I think of asking the Captain to allow it to be put into the cuddy. It would be so much cooler. The ladies expressed a little disappointment at my violin not being forthcoming. The meet me by Moon Light was not attended, or the appointments kept quite so punctual as on former occasions. I am the only one on board who can accommodate them with The White Cockade, the Trumpet etc. This Evening it was resumed at 8 pm and continued with much Spirit until ¼ to 9 when the Cap't wished a discontinuance as the Infant of one of the Passengers was dead. It had not been well many weeks and will be buried tomorrow, further particulars at the time and place. One of our best Cats kills today. Being 2nd we have now only one left, a large Blk and Wht Tom. It seldom leaves the hold as there are many rats. I wish we could get something to expiate the cockroaches.

Friday Nov 23rd

At 7 oclock a.m. enjoyed a Bathe. From the refreshing feeling produced and the color that I am told I had coming I am inclined to think it will be very beneficial to my constitution. I shall therefore persevere with it and bathe every morning. This day at 12 mid Day we are 350 miles off the line. The squally weather we are now passing through hardly enabled us to say how many days it will be before we cross it. It is thought by some it will be on Monday. I name this particular as all are looking forward to the fun that usually takes placed upon that occasion, when permitted by the Captain. There seems a diversity of opinion respecting it. The Sailors say he will, while others less favourable to it think otherwise. At 3 pm the funeral of Mary Ann Mumby aged 4 months took place. The service was well read by Mr Lasewood, the Captain, Doctor and 1st Mate being present, also Father his Brother and nearly all the Passengers. All labour of the Ships Crew was suspended for the time and great solemnity was observed quite as much as if it had taken place in the Church Yard of its birth place. I was rather surprised at Dancing being permitted upon the Poop this Evening. I thought the Cap'n out of respect to deceaseds Father would have had it postponed for at least one Evening. But from an enquiry I made I learnt that it had been spoken of but not thought necessary from its being so young. Doubtlessly had it have been an adult such amusement would not have taken place. 4 Country dances with 1st Set of Quadrille introduced us to the close of another day and at 10 oclock I partook of my scanty meal of cake and Effervescent draught. At 11 turned in for the night. I should think at least 30 slept upon the deck I do not sancion such proceeding and therefore never avail myself of that place for taking repose. A passenger was telling me the other day of the danger of sleeping upon deck. A relation of his that left England for Australia a short time since, when nearly there was missing in the morning at Breakfast time. It was named to the Captain, when he ordered all hands aft, and call over the names it was assertained to be too true. From what could be learned from one of the Passengers, he was last seen upon a Hen Coop on deck close by the side of the ship. It was thought a sudden lurch turned him over into the sea during the night when he sank to be seen no more alive.

Saturday Nov 24th

The early part of this day was cheerful and pleasant considering how near we are to the line. I consider it cool and not half so hot as I anticipated but I am told that were weather and the sun nearly over us as it now is, I should perhaps be afforded an opportunity to complain of the heat. It is the breese then I suppose enables us to bear it with pleasure for nothing really can be more delightful. The Business of the Ship progresses rapidly and without unpleasantness of any kind. The Sailors are a quiet, level and sober company of Men. There has only been two cases of Drunkenness amongst them. One was known to the Cap't as the man was obliged to go to the wheel being his turn. The other was not as he was soon put to Bed by his Messmates. The Carpenter has been engaged during the past week making Yards or Cross Timbers that support the Sails also Mizen Mast the intention being to make this Barque into a Ship Sails are also in state of great forwardness. I may hear tell you the difference between a Barque and a Ship as they are called by the builders. The former carries Two large Masts, Middle and Fore with that one at stern which mast carries the Driver and Gaff Topsale only. A Ship has 3 large masts alike and each Rig'd out in the same manner, with 4 sails upon them. It is thought that another month will suffice to complete the alteration. The mizen or first mast will carry mizen top sail, Top gallant and Mizen Royal.

The manner in which Christmas day and New years Eve is to be spent had become a subject of conversation. It is rumoured that the Captain has said he intends treating us with a little fresh mutton, one or two of the sheep kill'd. We have 5 very fine animals on board but Two would hardly supply a joint however small to each mess. Our Pudding for that days consumption is already made and requiring only to be warmed, one of Warminster manufacturing, being indebted to Mrs Brodrib for it. This Afternoon occasional showers though not very heavy. The orison [horizon] several times was dark and indicative of Squalls or heavy rains, but we fortunately escaped. The Sun set unusually splendid. On two or three occasions if has been very grand but this Evening it was unusually beautiful and I cannot refrain from making a remark upon its appearance. You have seen a fine sunset many times in England but I can assure you what I ever saw scarcely bears a comparison to that of a Setting Sun at Sea. Looking around, our vessell appearing the centre of the Circle (the orison). The Suns Gold rays shone upon about 3 parts of it, and in the fore ground formed the Appearance of High Black rocks projecting out and rising to a point into the sea. In the middle of these Rocks was an opening through which rays of brilliant light shone forth with awfull splendour giving the appearance of a deluge of waters. On various parts were to be seen light clouds as sunken islands and dark places upon them representing Farm and other Houses nearly gone or engulfed in the devouring elements. It reminded me of prints I have seen representing the great deluge. It attracted much notice and very many were the comparisons made to it. What tended to make it remarkable was its wide extent along the orison.

The weary Sun hath made her golden set
And by the ruddy brightness of the clouds
Gives them a goodly day tomorrow (Shakespeare I believe)

This morning I made our first cake, used all Butter some sugar, flour, raisins and water, and had it not have been baked too much it would have been nice enough for any thing. I gave my Rum for another share and hope it will last me all the following week as I cannot eat the biscuits. At 2 past seven the concert commenced and I annex one of our programmes which shall suffice. It is copied exact from the one sent to the captain.

Asiatic Concert

The Committee Submit their Programme to the notice of Cap Roskell and Passengers [and] hope the following Galaxy of Talent will meet with their entire approbation.

Part 1st.

Overture	By the Band
Catch "Grey Sand"	by Mrs Dunn and the Misses Neald
Song 3 Ages of Love	Mr W.Neads [? Or Miss W. Neald?]
The Pope he leads etc	Mr Salter
As I those scenes etc	Miss
Kiss and be Friends	Mr Broom
The Banks O'Doon	Mr Markill
Where Are these happy days	Mrs Dunn
Maggie Lauder	by the Colonel
A place in my memory	Mr Heron
Recitation From Henry 5th Shakespeare	Mr Winterton
Song Oh the sad sea wave	Miss Nealds
Adventure of Jonathan Jonah Goliah	by the Celebrated Mr Brown

Part 2nd

The Standard Bearer	MrWilmot [Willimott]
I love the merry sunshine	Miss Norris
The Wife's Dream	Mr Hawkes
How shall I woo thee	Mrs Laseward
Meet me by Moonlight	Mr Finnis
Present to the Queen	Mr Broom
Ned Button the Bold Privateer	Mr Simpson
A Popular Song	Mrs Garsed
The song of the shirt	Mr Winterton
Louise	By the funny man

Finale God save the Queen by the Company

In consequence of the length of the programme the performance will commence at

7 oclock precisely
Saturday Nov 26 1849
Vivat regine et principae

Passed off with the appearance of general satisfaction. Partook of a little biscuit cheese and water on retirement for the night. The water I must here name is most dreadfully bad both in smell and taste. The taste returns to ones mouth long after it is drank. Beastly I assure you and likely to be worse. Would that I had brought a filter. I would gladly give 20/- for the use of a [-] remainder of the voyage. I hope no one who reads this will think of leaving England without one.

Sunday Nov 25th

How pleasant would be a walk this morning to a country church at a distance of 4 or 5 miles. The delightfullness of the weather invites us most pressingly and - but alas I forget we are in the midst of the South Pacific Ocean - It is indeed the heat of a Tropical Sun. A Heavy Shower delayed a quarter of an hour our Church Service. It was a desirable cooler for the atmosphere. Rained Twice while the service was been performed but not to compell a discontinuance. The Text was from the 7 Chapter of Judges 15 Verse. The meeting was well attended and all attention manifested. A new article was introduced for dinner call'd Preserved Potatoes, a most excellent substitute and are served up mashed. They look uncooked, like scraps in the leaving after lard is made. The color is not good but taste passable. Some fresh or even good tasted salt butter would be a desirable addition. The Evening Service was at the usual time and place and Lecture the remaining part of the Mornings. At 10 retired to seak a bottle thrown over board this afternoon at 3 oclock enclosing a sheet of paper upon which was written Latitude 3.27 N Longitude 25.11 W. Signed by 14 of the Passengers and directed to Lloyds, London.

Tired natures sweet restorer, balmy sleep,
He like the world, his ready visit pays,
Where fortune smiles, the wretched he forsakes
On balmy pinion flies the bed of woe
And lights on lid unsullied with a tear

Young

Monday Nov 26th

At 2 past 6 made my appearance on deck for my bathe. A slight breeze blowing, making 7 knots. The increased motion of the vessell still trys my poor inside. The little barrell organ at work again. I am not by myself complaining, thats one comfort, as the felon said when he had company on the Gallow. The Hold cleaned out this morn'g and a scene of bustle ensued. The Upper Deck strewed with open Boxes, Packages of all sorts, kinds and description being turned out. I particularly noticed many persons with Ham, Bacon etc brought out of Boxes, wraped in brown paper. The consequence is turned rafty and in some instances full of maggots, and smells awfull. Over board it went, the same with cheese. Bringing of such articles is very desirable and I would have made a slight provision had I have known it, but then it must be managed in a difference to the above. Perishable articles should be packed separate in a Box or cask by themselves so as when brought up from the hold sufficient of every thing may be taken from it to last the time until the Box comes up again and all such packages etc should be marked Glass with Care Wanted upon the voyage, as it would go into a different part of the Ship and be used very different. I mean not knocked about so much. Matt dust Bran or Sawdust should be used to keep all dry, and I believe the damp does not get through. Potatoes is a capital article as they can be baked and make good lunches. As for bottles of Pickle Cabbage or any cheap mixture is most delightfull and a ready sale. Ginger, Nutmegs and all spice, Baking Powder, Currants, Raisins, Candied Peel, and the like, in short anything that can be afforded in small quantities, would serve to render this domicile a Palace not a Prison.

Tuesday Nov 27th

Bright are the Beams of the Morning Sky And bright is the suns golden ray

Wednesday Nov 28th

Engaged this morning first job washing out a shirt and then a little reading. All today peaceable and making good passage. Ships Crew busy preparing Sails for contemplated alteration and Carpenter making Top Mast. Many persons would be inclined to think that at Sea when the Sails did not require attention and all is proceeding straitforward and comfortable that sailors have little to do. It is indeed quite otherwise. They always seem busy and have a happy nack of making a little job appear large and last a long time, not however when they are changing the sails or making any alteration at the Command of the Captain or 1st or 2nd Mate. For then all is dispatch and noise or else they get one two or three heartyd - ns, - swearing seems a part and parcel of a salor conversation. I do not think I ever heard two talking together 3 minutes without an oath or something to it. They have a variety of peculiar expressions applyed to all subjects and used at any time without any application or reference to the subject under discussion.

Thursday Nov 29th

(This should be as Thursday Dec 6th)
Very little occured this morning requiring or affording me subject for comment. Employed myself Reading. Walked about chatting to one and another. Sitting about untill ones bones acke and ready to pot through the skin. I would recommend every one coming out to provide themselves with a portable seat. There are many on board,

but most of them very slight made, fancy article more for ornament than use, such that if I were to set down in them at all hasty I should go to the ground. Rough and strong as Mr Gill recommended my outfit to be, I have seen since leaving England in how many instances his judgement too was at fault, as also advice ill timed and useless. All moved on quietly until past 12, when was seen on our starboard

> *"A sail, a sail a promised prise to hope,*
> *Her nation Flag how speaks the telescope*
> *No prize alas, but still a welcomed sail*
> *Her blood red signal glitters in the gale,*
> *Yes she is ours A home returning bark,*
> *Blow fair thou breeze, she anchors ere tis dark"*
>
> \- Byron

In about half an hour from that time we first saw her she was along side us. She hoisted her flag and found to be one of "old Englands Hope." All was now confusion and surging about. Those that had not a letter written employed themselves, as hard as they were able in the hopes of sending by the approaching ship. Some like myself were contented to write a few lines. Others could scarcely be persuaded to leave off to take their dinner. The meat was not done with before it was said she was alongside I had just time to clear the Table and divide our pudding and then hastened upon deck with letter in hand. A few short minutes only elapsed before I again had proof that disappointments are the lot of Man. It proved to be the barque *Clio* of Swansey and bound for Quebec. Some were so exasperated that they through their letters over board. I did not do so myself thinking that it would be far better policy to put it away as a sort of reserve and use it on some future occasion when there was the same prospect of having my dinner as at this time. No dancing this evening Mr Meckney [McKechnie] being so very ill and laying exactly under were we dance, and the violin is played.

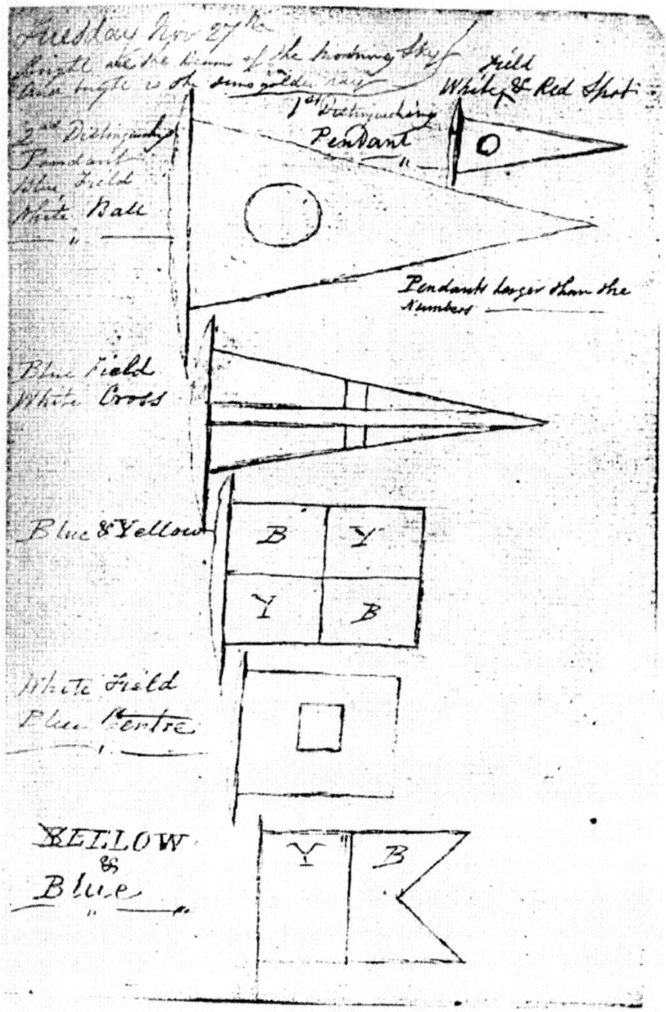

Pennants and Flags
drawn in James' Diary

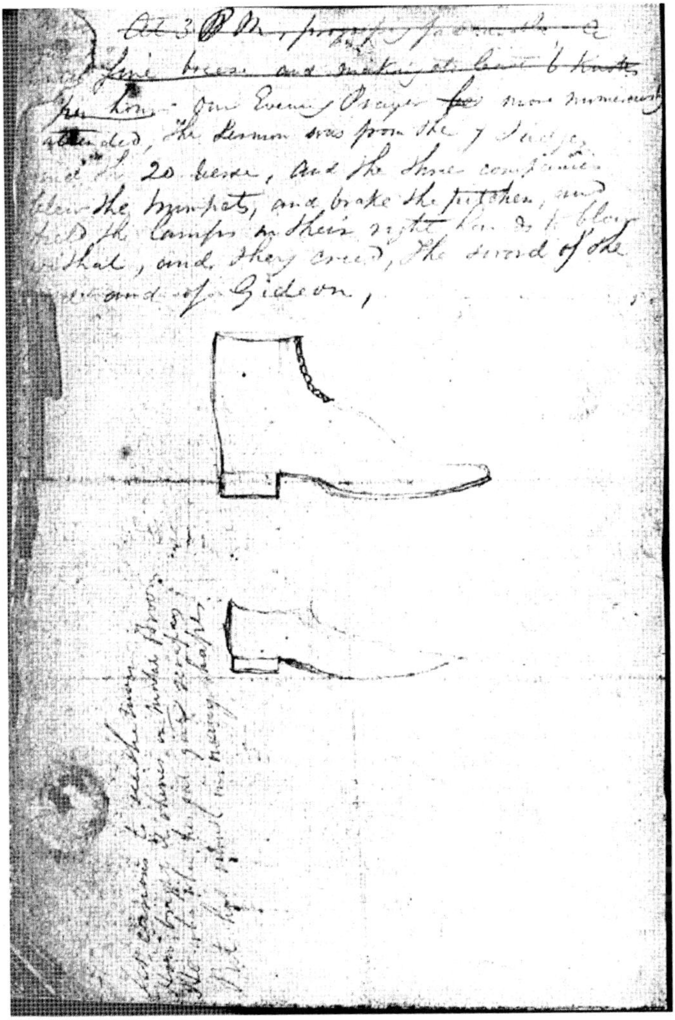

Boot and Shoe
drawn in James' Diary

Friday Nov 30th

This is wrong, must be Friday Dec 7th

This morning before I arose information was brought to my Cabin that Mr Meckney was no more, that he died at ½ past 12 last night. For several days I had noticed a great change, but did not think from what I had before seen in others that his end was so near. He was a Young Man about the middle stature and next birthday would have been 21. He has a Mother and Sister living at Bow London, and he left them to proceed to Launcester, Van Diamon Land, for the benefit of his health. His Brother is living there. He was known to a young man Mr Ellison the only person on board and by him waited upon with the greatest kindness and attention everything being done that circumstances would permit. It was evident to all that he could not under any ordinary circumstances out live the voyage and an oppion was expressed by many that they were quite at a loss to guess what his Friends could be thinking of to send him thus away to die upon the ocean. He was committed to the deep this morning at ½ past 10. The body was sowed up quite tight in canvass, with 14lbs of old Iron in a bag attached to the feet outside the canvass. The corpse laid during the time the burial service was being read covered with the Union Jack, and the Boxes supporting the plank the Body laid upon covered with the pendant Flag. I may here tell you that this Flag is used at sea to signalise with another Ship to tell them whereabouts they intend taking up their Quarters or when going to any particular place. For instance supposing this Vessel was to see another ship at such a distance that they could not speak but only through a glass see a Flag hoisted, and they wished to tell them that they were going to Sydney, they would first hoist the Pendarans Flag and underneath another that would give the name or number and by their referring to a Book, all ships have a book alike, they would immediately see the desired information. Sometimes there are as many as 6 flags up at a time. It is astonishing with what correctness information is thus transmitted. Mr Lasewood as before read the burial service and the Capt took the clerks place. At 12 a Sale took place of all deceases Perishable articles and which fetched a good price. Mr Barker Linen Draper acted as auctioneer. He made his will some few days since before the Captain and Doctor. His money (which was but very little) and Clothes was left to his Brother to be forwarded upon the arrival of the vessel. I subjoin a list of the Articles and Prices which they fetched just to give you an idea what such things are sold for on board and leave you to guess wheather it would not be a speck to bring out a tolerable stock with the idea of turning them into money. I am quite certain that if I had a sufficient quantity of the right articles I might easily make a profit enough to pay my passage money. I would recommend a person before laying in a Stock to assertain which stores the Ship intends to carry and the prices of each. They would then be able to work upon tolerable sure grounds. A few small biscuits 7d, wine glasses, tumbler, both small and common 1/6 sweetmeats 1/3 sugar and can 5d Ink and Stand 8d, Pint and half Bottle of Cirup of some kind or other 2/6 Very small pot of Currant Jelly held about half Pint 1/3 Do. Do. ¼ Pint or the smallest Pot I should think made 7d. Pint Bottle of mix'd Pickles (1/- at home) 1/11. Pot of Preserved Gooseberries about pint and half 3/7 Pot of Black Jam not larger than my own 2/6 Same size Preserved Quince 2/4 Can of Arrow Root hold about 2 pints 3/- ¾ Pint Bottle Lemonade Powder not full sold at Plymouth 2/- 3/8 A Nassau Bottle of Lime Guice 3/3 Bottle of Port 1½ Pint 3/3 another Do 3/6 (The cheapest lot being very good) 1 Gallon Stone Jar 1/6 Total amount [£]1-17-6 and plenty of Bidders For if these had been 5 times the quantity, it would have met a ready sale. I was quite surprised at their eagerness. I would not have given half the price for any which sold with the exception of the Port wine, which I was told was worth in England 5/-, being first rate.

Saturday Dec 1st

More noise and drunkenness this day on board than any since here we have been The Captain was obliged to come down twice, first to the serv't of the male Passengers (Huntington). This uproar began by his thrusting a hole in the bottom of one the Passengers cans because it leaked and he had some little trouble to swab up the water. After much noise talking, swearing and all but fighting, some one stepped to the Cap't. His appearance soon silenced them, particularly when Irons were talked of. The next row was between two of the most peaceable men here on board when sober. They were setting together drinking etc all the fore part of the afternoon, but liquor got the better of their judgements, memory and every thing else and not being able to find anyone willing to have a quarrell with them must needs set to by themselves. They drank 3 bottles of ale, Double allowance of Rum (Saturday and Sunday Grog being served out this day for the first and will - owing to this spree - be for the last time). 12 Bottle of Rum besides. The quarrel lasted for an hour when it grew to such a hight that the Captain was fetched. They insulted him, 1st and 2nd Mate, and was ordered, Brown to his Cabin under escort or guard of one the midshipmen until 4 next morning, Ryan likewise guarded upon the Poop until the same hour.

Sunday Dec 2nd

Washed and dressed for the day by 6 am took my seat upon the Poop. The conversation turned upon the difference of weather in England and that which we are now situated. The 2nd of December doubtless with you is wet, cold and dreary, and G[rea]t Coats required to go to Church in. We are more inclined to complain of the Heat and can sit about all day without our Coats or Hats on. Brown and Ryan, the transgressors of yesterday, made full apologies to the Captain etc for misconduct of yesterday. The Services held at the usual hour. The Sermon was from the 6 Chap of Judges and 16 verse. Employed reading this morning one of Rev. B. W. Noals sermons lent me by Charles. A short nap this afternoon for the first time since I have been on board, the effects I suppose of too good a dinner. The Evening discourse was the concluding half read in the morning.

Monday Dec 3rd

No dancing to night and the Captain was solicited to have the Concert held this evening not taken place Saturday, but he refused owing to the late misconduct, and it is thought that he will not allow another concert or other priviledge for some period. I had pointed out to me for the first time The Magellan Clouds. They are two small ones and nearly close together. The latitude we are now in one is on our right and the other the left of our Bows, and in appearance not unlike the Milky Way.

Tuesday Dec 4th

Little opportunity is afforded me this morning to furnish you with ought that I could imagine amusing or instructive. As Pat says there is nothing moving but stagnation that may really be said of our situation. At dinner today we were obliged to throw ourselves upon the generosity of our Mess Mates. Mast[er] Charles coming down the Hatch way contrived to step into the hold and throw our Boulli Soup all over himself and away went our dinner and we may as well have thrown away our appetites at the same time. All we had besides was boild beef of which we never can eat 2 mouthful at the best of time being so dreadfully hard and today it was no use to touch it Some were kind enough to spare us a little soup and we patched up our appetites tolerably well, all things being considered.

Thursday Dec 6th

This is for Thursday 29th last month Entered. See preceding week Nov 29

A sail ahead this morning and continued untill the setting Sun veiled all in the darkness of night. The morning was cool and lovely and the sun rose bright and cloudless. I borrowed an amusing Book, sat about reading. After dinner washed out 4 Silk Hdkss [handkerchiefs]. Found things had suffered much from damp and one or two spotted amongst them. I had been obliged to put my cake into one and other things as well to keep them as dry as possible. A very important event took place this morning which I cannot allow to pass unnoticed. It had so long been look upon as a friend in need and afforded me a scanty meal many times when fasting otherwise would have been the fashion and I may truly say it was never taken out of my Box and cut without thinking of the Maker and Giver, you my dear Mother. The Cake, I allude to, of which I this morning I eat the last piece. It kept good to the last, and would have continued so for another month had I chosen. Bought some Pictures and Books this afternoon paid for same 1/-. The Silk Hdkfs I have just alluded to as being spotted with damp etc. were not part of those I bought in Bath and which you may remember seeing. I had a greater bargain at Plymouth. There I bought five at 1/3 each. The others were 1/2½ but nothing like the quality of my last purchase. It is astonishing how the sea air and water spots and removes the color from ones wearing apparel. My coat in two or three places has lost its color or rather is turned, by the ropes rubbing against it at times when I have been helping to pull, quite yellow. I imagine yourself with others would be ready to say it is impossible for that coat, the little Jersey coat, to loose any of the color that had already been lost some years ago also. It is replaced [?] I now to a certainty and when I land at Adelaide ought to place it in its old age in good keeping as the reward of long and good servitude.

Saturday Dec 8th

Rather showery this morning and the air thereby considerably cooled. Engaged like many more Captains of' Messes making cake and Duff for tomorrow. Every thing progressing most favourable, nothing of any moment intervening to break through the monotonous of our daily routine of Business. I have not as yet told you how the time is kept on board so as to be known by the whole Ships Company. There is a large Bell in the centre of the breast of the Poop exactly over the middle window of the Cuddy, that is struck by the midshipman on duty every half hour. The number of strokes (the Capper being used) denotes the hour. And the hours are kept in the following way. 8 strokes or "Bells" as they are called announces 12 midday. At ½ past 12 1 Bell is given. At 1 oclock 2 Bells and so on in like manner increasing 1 Bell every half hour until 4 oclock pm when it has come to 8 Bells. Then comes what is termed the Dog Watches, an explanation of which I must likewise give you. In the first place the reason these watches kept is to give by such arrangement 7 watches instead of 6 which otherwise would be the case. At ½ past 4 1 Bell, 5 oclock 2 Bells ½ past 5 3 Bells, 6 4 Bells then commencing again 1 Bell at ½ past 6, 2 at 7, 3 at ½ past 7 At 8 is struck 8 Bells and so on through every 24 hours. 8 o'clock comes in its turn again for the Eight Bells. The Concert not permitted this Evening, supposed to be in consequence of the misconduct which unfortunately took place the preceding Saturday afternoon. Dancing for an hour and a half and kept up in the most animated style, much to the annoyance of my fingers and arms which cried out sadly.

Sunday Dec 9th

7 o clock am. Much cooler this morning, a strong breeze blowing from 1 until 4 am. The wind shifting and blowing our direct course. We are making full 8 knots and at about the distance of 30 miles from the Island of Trinidad lying to our left. It was distinctly to be seen, appearing like a dark Cloud rising above the orison and I should not have noticed it or thought it more than a cloud had it not have been pointed out to me and my noticing that it did not move as the clouds were then doing. The prospect of our voyage being somewhat shortened by this unexpected fresh breeze springing up much encourages us and cheers our drooping spirits. Service held as usual but disappointed no Sermon. Sang only twice, 4 first verses of the 19th and 20th Psalm. I attended the Afternoon Service but the heat between decks made one feel most sleepy and I had some difficulty preventing myself being overtaken by it. If I had drop'd into a nap the movement of the vesselle would have capsized and spread me upon the floor. No Church Service held this Evening there being such a strong indication of Squally weather. If it had have been commenced the rain would not have permitted it continuance. The Sailors are making preparations for a storm, Shortening sail and being busy with much noise. I have not seen more than one or two large fish but those off Cape Madeira, a Circumstances which has somewhat surprised me. About 3 pm I happened to be standing upon the forecastle and was the first to notice at least 20 Porpoise (or sea pigs as the Sailors call them) playing beneath our Bows. I sung out to some of the Sailors, when one procured his Harpoon and took his station upon the Dolphin Spike, a projecting Piece of timber or pole standing out from the

Bow of the vessell and the farthest point out or rather the nearest to the water of any in the vessell. When the waves are running high it dips in them, but did not succeed in catching one.

Monday Dec 10th

The rain commenced last Evg about 9 oclock and lasted until 4 this morning. It was very heavy and many buckets of fresh water were caught. The weather very much cooler rather inclined to be cold. I had not been in Bed last night more than an hour before the water came through the upper deck upon my Bed in 4 different places. I remained in my Bunk as long as I thought there was a chance of sleeping there the night, but the rain continuing with unabated violence and my patience was at last exhausted. I thought an hours amusement sitting up with my head nearly touching the ceiling and all but dark as pitch, holding a basin in one hand and Plate in the other, quite long enough for the first trial. So turned out and dressed myself. Our cabin was in a pretty considerable state of confusion and wet enough for anything. Two besides myself were obliged to turn out. Charley moved his Bed under the Table and I quietly put myself into his vacated bunk. The water had come through upon him but little, which I readily found a remedy for. So spreading my sheet and blanket, the only articles that were not soaked, turned in very comfortable for the night and enjoyed as good a sleep as I would ever wish for on board the *Asia*, as upon examination they turned out to be much worse than I had anticipated

Tuesday Dec 11th

Towards the morning the wind droped into a dead calm, as though wearied out by its own powerful exertions, those of the preceding day. For during the past 12 hours we have laid tossing about, if in motion proceeding towards our late homes, but certainly not making progress towards reaching the desired haven of our hopes Port Adelaide. It is surprising what a change will take place in a few hours as regards the appearance of the sea and state of the wind. Yesterday we were going 8 knots and today not one. I brought up my mattress towards getting it fit to lay upon once more but after 3 attempts failed, as the continued showers did not give us half an hours sunny weather the whole day. I am obliged to lay upon a borrowed Horse Rug, one of Charley's and as that scarcely covers the boards of my kneading Trough, I find it slightly inclined to be hard but healthy. At 8 pm tolerably clear and not raining. Received summons from my Master (Pro tem) the Captain to make my appearance upon the poop with violin, as they wished to join in the friendly dance. I obeyed the summons. I never go there with violin unless sent for by him or at his instigation, by which proceeding I anticipate not trespassing or making myself obnoxious or any anoyance to him. I had not been there longer than to give the time to choose partners and take their places for the country dance when down came the rain. All hastened under cover and went below. There is seldom anything to be done after the lamps are lit between decks particularly of a wet Evening besides Card playing, chess or raffling, so at a quarter before nine I layed up for the night and was pretty comfortable disposing myself towards sleep - I received one, two even 3 messages from the ladies to informing me they awaited the appearance of myself and violin. Twice sent word I was in bed and could not come and the 3rd and last time I called to my aid as an excuse suffering from a sore throat, which latter was accepted and I was let off promising that I would do double duty upon the next occasion.

8124 from Australia   2312 from the Cape

Wednesday Dec 12th

The morning cooler, very considerably so. The fine warm, and beautiful sunny weather seams to have bid us farewell for a time, I hope but for a short time only. Think many of us including myself will be obliged to take to wearing stockings again. It is now I think five or six weeks since I have had a pair on. The Parents of very few of the children allowed them to wear sox or stockings and a plan much to be recommended particular were the washing of them is so very inconvenient. The feet can be washed 20 times a day if thought necessary but not so with stockings and nothing could be worse in a close Cabin than a lot of Dirty clothes in a Bag. There is difficulty enough to keep the place sweet and fit for sleeping without such addition.

Thursday Dec 13th

At 4 am the crew were all aroused from their beds and put upon a hard days work raising the mizen mast. This during the day was completed 2 of the Yards up and 1 sail, the mizen Top Sail. The weather still continues getting cooler and the sun hid from us the whole day. Did not feel quite well this morning. Obliged to have recourse to my brandy bottle, sampled its contents and I finding it had lasted tolerably well, now rather more than 2 months. Dancing as usual this evening. Sent down the mizen top mast and commenced getting down the mizen rigging for the purpose of converting the *Asia* into a Ship.

Friday Dec 14th

Awoke somewhat better in health after enjoying a good nights repose. Still colder and raining several times during the day. The sun withholding its cheerful rays. We had any thing but a pleasant time of it. A wet day on board is miserable, penned down below amidst so much noise and uproar as there always is when any quantity of the Passengers are compeled to be between Decks. When the Hatches are nearly covered over, which is the case when it rains hard, it is so dark that one cannot even see to read. You may give a pretty near guess the amusement upon such occasion.

Saturday Dec 15th

Exceedingly hot and uncomfortable during the night. Was awakened two or three times finding myself much too warm with a disagreeable itching and which kept me awake for a half hour at a time. I have had it more or less for the past fortnight, caused I suppose by over heated blood We anticipate it will be much cooler as we round the Cape. This Morning was very different weather to what we have had for the past two days. The Sun rose bright and shedding its peaceful and benign rays over the wide expanse of ocean. The breeze is fresh, invigorating cool and delightful and several times has the thought crept in, I trust we may have another such the day we are all spared to put foot upon the long looked for shore. This morning there was a considerable uproar between several of' the passengers, the Clerk and Attendant of the Stores. It had been discovered that short weights had been made in the Articles of Salt, Potatoes and Sugar in particular, etc. One party who happened to be possessed of Weights and Scales detected it and three or four made a regular stand against the imposition. It was settled after a good deal of argument and the deficiencies made up. I would advise to bring scales and a few weights as it might be the means of keeping the parties that serve out the stores honest and ensure the receipt of full allowance. A Funnell is also an indispensable article as it comes in for so many different purposes. The water becomes better and keeps sweeter in Glass Bottles with the cork left out than in any other vessell. The Articles enumerated in the list of Medical comforts are good, and would if distributed add much to the comforts of passengers, but such is not the case. For not one single thing is given out if it can by any possibility be done without. If any such as arrow root, oat meal etc etc is asked for there is so much difficulty in obtaining it that, without it really cannot be done with, many go away disgusted by having the difficulty and waiting so long for it.

Sunday Dec 16th

A short walk before Breakfast. Not a walk in the green fields over the rail road or around cop heath or Strole for an hour in the Garden as I was wont to do some 3 months back, but a half hours promenade upon the poop of the area in the very midst of the South Atlantic Ocean, a most excellent expedition and I could have made a no mean repast by an introduction to a table suitably spread. For such must I wait patiently another 2 months, when I hope to set down, to rise knowing that I have partaken of a breakfast, such knowledge at present not being permitted me The remains of Saturdays beef boiled to death and as hard as the knocker of Newgate, with biscuit and but little more than ½ a pint of tea was all that I could present to my ungodly to satisfy its demands. It may be supposed I arose but little the better for a ¼ of an hour spent at the Table de Dejeuner. Another as beautiful a day as was ever spent in the midst of these great waters. The sea with scarcely a ripple and a gentle breeze stealing softly over its wide expanse and during the afternoon taking us along 5 knots but the morning varying from 1 to 3. During the night it was almost a calm. Service as usual this morning but thinly attended many not yet up. The Psalms sung were the 95th and 105th and the Sermon from 6th of Judges and 34 verse. After Dinner from which I made up for my poor breakfast I felt much inclined to nap so turned into my bunk and for the first time indulged myself with a couple of hours sleep, awoke refreshed and comfortable and walked the deck for an hour or so previous to partaking of the water bewitched. Tea or liquid of any kind comes acceptable as the warm weather and salt provisions makes us very thirsty. The Evening Service was much better attended than the Morning. Sang three times and the sermon was from the same text as before and the concluding part of morning Lecture. I have not yet mentioned that nearly all the sailors take their seats at Prayer dressed in their best or rather I suppose I should say their clean clothes. What brought more particularly under my notice this morning was one of them coming forward to help get ready for divine service, in his dirty clothes. The Captain reprimanded him very severely and from what was said on both sides I doubt very much if there is repetition next Sabbath morning. The men all appear very happy and cheerful and it is pleasing to see what an attempt is made even by them to keep holy day. Sailors, with the exception of Colliers, are the roughest and most unpolished race of beings I am acquainted with. I have more than once been tempted to laugh to see 3 or four sitting together in a row each turning over a quid of tobacco and useing for a spittoon one of the buckets. They pay great attention, and I really believe they would rather go without their Plum Duff which they have only upon Sundays rather than not have the day kept in the manner it is. They employ their time principally in reading some (as they call it) good story Book. On many occasions I have seen 3 or 4 laying together in the fore Castle, one reading aloud, the others all attention. The close of another earthly Sabbath is dawning upon us. The sun has set with all the refulgance of a summers eve and the hour warns me that I must ere long betake myself from deck My thoughts, as on the present occasion, often turn to England Home and Friends. With the beautiful weather we have this day had, how I should enjoy the day spent with you in Bath, not that I have passed it here altogether miserable. We cannot be decidedly dull and mallenary [melancholy?] and I trust at all times I shall enjoy the priviledge of a Sabbath whether worshiping in the briny ocean or the quiet of an inland village.

Hail the Sabbath as a boon
The poor man's day
On other days the man of toil is doom'd
To eat perhaps his joyless bread alone
Or share his frugal meal with her he loves
For love to him is heaven and heaven is love
For on this day, embosomed in his home
With Partner share with heartfelt joy
And give their thanks to God.

["Hail Sabbath thee I hail the poor man's day" James Grahame "The Sabbath"]

Monday Dec. 17th .

This day weather, as before described, fully equally, if not surpassing in brightness, Freshness and Delightfulness any previously one depicted. The mornings engagement divided between reading and filling up Box for the reception of lamp used upon the Poop for me to see my music by for playing to our nightly dance Hithertoo one of the Junior Midshipmen have been obliged to remain with me to hold on the lamp, as the rolling of the vessel would capsize it, and it also requires to be covered up upon 3 sides, otherwise daselling the Eyes and interfering with the man at the wheel and the dancing is under. Unpleasant. The little light I obtained only serving to balk, not sufficient to light up efficiently that part of the Poop used for dancing which is immediately in front of the Mizen Mast. The afternoon passed of with its wontened cheerfullness, and an opportunity presenting itself to purchase a few magasines I embraced it, paying for the same 1/- turning over the pages of which I was much amused and somewhat consoled for I find that if I cannot obtain a situation in my old trade there is yet a chance left for the rough and ready life of the Bushman. The quotation now given if true is no less very remarkable but unfortunately I place no more belief in it than in numerous other Baron Machauson [Munchausen] tales I have before met with.

"In the Bush" says the author of the *Working Man's handbook to Australia*, "the Shepherds class consists of the most heterogeneous materials. Within 10 miles of the place were I lived I remember, as shepherds, one apothecary, one lawyer's clerk, one counting house clerk, three sailors, one tailor, one Jew, one Portuguese sailor, one native of Ceylon, one Australian black, one barman, one Gentleman's son brought up to no business at all, one New Zealand merchant, who had been burnt out, and a second Portuguese who could not understand a word of English, one person late a lieutenant in the Hon. East India Company's Service and one Gipsy. These parties were all either shepherding or hulkeeping and the Gentleman's Son, the Jew and the Barman made the best Shepherds of the lot. A few miles further off, at a friends station there was a black fiddler and a Dancing Master. A large sheep owner told me that he would sooner take a Sailor who hardly knew the head from the stern of a sheep or a clerk who had been in an office all his life, than an English bred shepherd."

Another specimen of the tricks practised upon the unwary while passing through ships probationary state, or Ship life in other words, occured this Eve'g and the writer of this unfortunately was amongst the sufferers. Our tea kettle, or Pot as it is called, was brought down, and placed upon the Table full of hot water with the usual quantity of tea in it. Myself and Charley were gone to the

Cabin for our Tin Pannicans (or Cups which hold a Quart). The Young Man that brought the tea down had likewise left the Table for his cup or sugar and in the absence a quantity of pepper was slipped into it. I need scarcely remark, all was turned over board and for this Evening we were compelled to make a draught of water with slice of Pork suffice for Tea, alias Supper, or the last meal for the day. It would not be out of place here to remark that should you or any one into whose hands this may fall come out in a vessel of this description (a mixed class of Passengers I allude to which of course it would be) lay it down as a rule, one absolutely necessary, keep to yourself as much as possible, keep what you have on board with you to yourself, and as much out of sight and knowledge of the passengers as possible, or else they will be begging or borrowing all day long. Keep all moveables under lock and key and Key in your Pocket, or do not call anything your own out of your sight. Pilfering or taking what you require for your use, is looked upon not as an act deserving and calling forth censure, but as a matter of course, and when an article is gone the common practice is to supply the loss the first opportunity no consequence from where or who is the sufferer. It is surprising what bearfaced acts of mislaying dayly occur. You lay any article (Articles that you cannot replace) upon the Table, such as Knife, Fork Spoon or even dinner plate, no distinction as to kind, value or discription. Turn your back and you may bet 10 to 1 on your return something is gone. The afforesaid appoligy for Tea being concluded at eight oclock some Poetical effusions which had been received during the past week by the Captain were placed into the hands of our leader of the Concerts and by him (seated upon the Capson) read aloud for the amusement and information of the whole company. They were all more or less intended to take off (altho not dicidily offensive), one or more of the passengers. Some of the courting couples came in for their share, Captain, 1st and 2nd mate not exempted, and during the reading which occupied nearly half an hour their being not less than from 15 to 20 pieces, many were the bursts of applause, much laughter, and not a little fun created by such attempts at punning. Anything is a help to pass away the long hours and while nothing vicious or personal is resorted to, much merriment may be expected. I have as yet only been able to procure one which I subjoin. I am greatly in hopes of procuring some if not all the others, and which if such should be the case I will give them most undoubtly. Immediately after the readings were concluded I was summoned for the dance. It was kept up most spiritedly, Quadrille and Country dance following each other in rapid succession, terminating at about a quarter past 10. All seeming pleased with an Evening passed in so rational a manner and as I left the Poop, wishing them good night, many were the thanks I received for my humble contribution to the nights hillarity.

Hen Coop Confessions by An Imprisoned Chanticleer.
No. 1 Ye loves of Mast'r James & Miss Thyrza
Tune John Anderson my Joe

McKenzie that I love you
I've gien ye proofs enough
I've made you bouiller pie
And gien ye lots of Duff
I've nightly danced wi' you Mac
While others I've refused
And if you dont propose Mac
I'm really not well used.

2
Miss Nealds you make me proud Miss
And quite a happy lad
For since I've danced with you Miss
I've really been half mad
And when I've walked about Miss
My arm supporting thine
I've very often wished Miss
That you were really mine.

3
Oh gin ye speak the truth Mac
And dinna tell a lee
For you like Annie Laurie
I'd lay me down and dee
I'd strive both night and day Mac
My bonnie lad to please
And though you're precious soft Mac
I never would you tease.

4
No rubs about my softness Miss
Such strains no longer flow
For now from off the main mast
They call me Romeo
And if you'll marry me Miss
When we reach Adelaide
I'll aye be kind to you dear
My bonny English maid.

5
I'll readily consent Mac
For to become your wife
A name I've struggled hard for
The most years of my life
And when that I'm a bride Mac
From you neer haste awa
To tell the glorious news Mac
In the cuddy to mama

Composed by Mr A Simpson

Tuesday Dec'r 18th

No alteration of weather and to compensate for other information I will give you another of the Songs before allowed and which was used on the occasion.

To the Quiz on Board the *Asia*

Where are you going that rhyme is so rife
To lead a wandering Bushranger's life
If so bring your scrawling stuff to an end
and to the devil such trumpery send

2
You will never reach Parnassus great height
Though your fancy may take a wandering flight
You will never make a Shakespear or Hood
Your poetical ideas will neer be so good.

3
Confine yourself to the sphere you are in
For oft time folly leads to sin
Think of your future Bushman's life
Nor weary us with love or strife

4
Then leave off your evil futile appeals
And dance Sir Roger or even Scotch Reels
And shew yourself a little more on the Poop
And not to such Paltry ideas to stoop.

Asia Dec 14th / 49

Dancing again as usual. Played previous to being sent for to the Poop about 1 hour for the Sailors. We had some fine fun. This is the 2nd or 3rd time they have had a dance to themselves. As soon as I have finished Tea they are on to me for the Scrape.

Wednesday Dec 19th

Continuance of beautiful fine weather and proceeding exceedingly well on our journey. The Boxes from fore and main holds out again this morning. I looked to mine, did not disturb any thing. Found by a top Garment or two that all was right and nothing mildewed so corded it up again for the last time I hope during the voyage. At an Early hour a sail was discried at a considerable distant just visible to the naked Eye. A Barque outward bound in sight all day but no chance even to get a word with her. Dancing as usual but rather later, nearly ¼ past 10 am before we broke up. They give me a regular warming. I do not get a rest between the dances of 10 minutes, my finger arms and shoulder acking much. They think nothing of dancing one Country dance half an hour, with a change of 3 tunes.

This is in praise of a young Sport christened "The Collegian" and words to the tune of The Old English Gentleman.

We sing you a fine new song that was made I'm told of late
Of a fine young English Student who had not an Estate
Who came to sea because he no longer at home could stay
So in the night he packed up and from London ran a way
This fine young English Student a Gent of the present time.
This fine young English Student a Gent of the present time.
2
He travelled fast and came on board the Asia at Plymouth lying
Where he soon began to strut about and the Girls was slyly eyeing
He talked of Hundreds and of thousands to pass the time away
And I'm sure that those who heard him, believed what he did say
This fine young English Student etc etc
3
With money in his pocket he thought to cut a dash
And sovereigns he spent as if they were merely trash
But sovereigns fly on board a ship as fast as those on land
Thus now this fine young Student as not one at his command
Like a fine young etc etc
4
And now about the deck he walks all seedy and forlorn
With short pipe stuck into his mouth from Evening until morn
Some say he has turned Poet his pockets for to heal
While others say it is not him but the man at the wheel
Oh this fine young English Student one of the Asia line

Thursday Dec 20th

This morning was informed by our Boatswan, one of the oldest sea faring men on board that he never remembers during the many voyages it has been his lot to take, such a continuation of fine weather. Not too warm, not unpleasantly hot in the sun, just the weather suited to our situation, weather made on purpose for us to set and lie about, taking everything easy & realising my anticipations to the letter, 4 Months holliday and wearing out the old Clothes. Fearing that my trowsers now in wear would perhaps not hold together another couple of months and being offered another pair for 3/- I imbraced the opportunity & took them. Also paid for map of England, 1848 26ins by 18ins. Paid for same Price 6d. Also made exchange toasted duff and jam for writing paper, ruled, which if spared to carry out my present situation, this journal will be written upon it. It is a good article and I think well adapted for such purpose. The Boxes &c from the fore Hold this day, and empty water casks removed and their places supplyed by others full. The Sailors very hard at work. A Box containing Apples, Onions and Potatoes opened this day for the first time. Out of a large Basket of beautiful apples not 10 were good for anything. The onions and potatoes would do tolerable well. There was two faults made and which caused the failure. In the first place the cover or lid did not fit down tight enough to keep out the cockroaches. There was just room enough at one end to let them in. The Box was literally swarming, Potatoes and Apples nearly eat up by them. In the second there was but little straw used, instead of being placed in layers with sound sawdust, or even dry straw between them would have been better. Early this Evening upon the Poop. The juvenals had there dance and some rare fun it was to see such a quantity of little Boys and Girls opping about. They were very much pleased and are promised a dance every Evening. Did not retire to bed before 12 oclock not sleeping and feeling very warm. About ½ an hour afterward a fight took place between 2 of the Youths. Three or four rounds sufficed to induce one to acknowledge himself beaten.

Friday December 21st

Did not sleep well, not closing my Eyes before 2 o'clock, and at 7, when I ought to be up and dressed for the day, I was fast asleep and had it not have been for shame and encouragement to bad habits would have remained until 12 o'clock. Engaged this morning assisting Mr McKenzie pack His Box of Clothes having taken all out to air. Made Cake and brushed my own Coats which I have kept, having a prospect of requiring them upon the voyage, under my mattress. Also bought Fine merino vest paid for which 2/6. This is the way the money goes. I continue to spend mine coins on board like the rest of us. Two sail in sight the whole of this day. This morning was allowed out an extra or rather an allowance of Flour, Suit and Rasins, for making Pudding upon Christmas day. Full quantities will be given out at usual time tomorrow morning so that there should be no interfering with the operation. And I have heard that instead of our Rum on that day we are to be supplied with Brandy.

A Calm this day scarcely a breath of air stirring. 1 or 2 knots is the very outside, a poor prospect of getting round the Cape by New Year's day.

Saturday Dec 22nd

This morning the Two Vessels in sight were near enough to signalize. One proved to be French the other a Danish. At 10 o'clock the Danish was near enough we were able to speak with, when Her Skipper informed us they were 40 days from Cadiz and bound to Calcutta. This afternoon both vessels soon away from us and at 5 pm were nearly out of sight. We therefore think it advisable to alter the name of our ship and call her The Regulator, all the other vessels going by it. Today was favoured with another Specimen of the Poetical genius on board this Regulator.

Epigrams on the Affections by the man at the wheel.

1

Sear not O time our youthful brows with furrows
Whilst of the loves of Faithfull and of Burrows
We chant, with songs of glee that joyful strain
As the good Asia ploughs the briny main.

2

Also on him, let Jove's relentless thunder burst
Who would from Winterton take Miss Longhurst
For these true loves, I oft did feel
While standing at my dog watch wheel.

3

Of all the youthful beaux I've seen,
There's none like little Turner
He loves the Irish maid Rooney
O may he never mourn her.

4

But see thou not my muse you loving pair
Charles Willimot the young - Eliza Dutton fair
O beardless Boy! Inconstant swain
Thou first did love the Fair Basan

5

Though last not least, although in love he tarries
Comes illustrious Smith who courts Miss Harris
But she, impatient of her loves delay
Rejects poor Smith and seeks another prey.

The concert this Evening as usual. I gave them one song not being able to remain there all the time. Engaged below, making my Sundays Pudding. I was called upon for a Second. By my non appearance called forth a wish from some of them.

Sunday Dec 23rd

If I may venture to name any alteration of the weather this morning it must be that of rather cooler, not cold, but rather fresher and what is usually expected when in this latitude, 1600 miles from the cape. The past week has been miserable slow coaching of it. The morning Prayer but thinly attended. We had an excellent discourse from 7th Judges and 8 verse, and the Lord said unto Gideon By the 3 Hundred men that lapped will I save you, and deliver the Midianites into thy hand and let all the people go every man into his place. At the conclusion of the service I walk'd the deck until dinner time when I partook of a hearty repast of Roast Beef and Plum Duff. At 3 pm progressing favourably, a fine breese and making at least 6 knots per hour. I sought retirement from the noise and the groups congregated gossiping upon deck (my general place of retirement is upon the spars upon the Jolly boat on the middle deck) to write a few lines in my Journal. I feel happy and very thankful for past mercies and the Sunday before Christmas awakens in my mind recollection of the past. Under what different auspicies I spent this day last year. I did not, I could not, have enjoyed the service of that day more. I was not less mindfull of favour past, or did I feel less inclination to trust Him for the future. How frequently do events occur, and changes take place while passing through this probationary state in which conspiciously appeared His watchful care and may be traced the protecting Hand Him who is Lord of the Sabbath. As Sabbaths roll on do the opportunities for prayer and thankfulness return and another occasion presents itself for silently pouring forth those strains of heartfelt gratitude to the author of our being and of every temperal and spirital mercies. Different indeed is the striving seen around me and how different now is the opportunity for watchfulness and public Prayer. Such events will not however altogether prevent but assist to retard and prolong thanksgiving. The Ships Company are engaged in various necessary duties upon the Sabbath though nothing more is done than absolutely necessary. I myself am even engaged and have my duties. Yet I cannot be prevented the enjoyment of silent prayer. In the words of Mongomery How beautiful is Prayer discribed It is the burthen of a sigh The Falling of a tear The upward glancing of an eye When none but God is near The simplest form of speech That Infant lips can try Prayer the sublimest strain that reach The Majesty on high.

I think of those at home, those I know in whose thought I myself so frequently pass. I cannot at all times prevent them wandering to my native shores. Many are my surmises as to the manner in which you are all engaged and what may be the passing events with you. With the pressing knowledge of boundless mercies of which I have been so many years the happy recipitant I would cry Oh God permit me a Sinner to offer Thee the tribute of my earnest heartfelt thanks for protection during past life but more particularly for thy watchful care during the past 2 months with other favours vouchsafed. I enjoy a few moments like these snatched from the busy scenes of this "Little World of Ours" and be able to recognise the hand of a heavenly Fathers love, poured forth from the fullness and in exhaustable source some welcomed blessing and which ought to fill our heart with unexpected joy. These are moment my dear Mother I would not barter or exchange for any wordly gifts, and such moments we are all assured those will enjoy who die happy in a Saviors love. Such moments eternity of heaven consists which we shall obtain if we walk aright. May I be helped to bear such constantly in view and lean upon the strong for strength, & trust to the merits and intercession of our Redeemer. Our Evening prayer more numerously attended. The Lesson was from the 7 Judges and the 20 verse And the three companies blew the trumpets, and brake the pitchers and held the lamps in their right hands to blow withal, and they cried, The sword of the Lord and of Gideon.

Tis curious to see the moon
How bright it shines on M[ortal?] Broom
He who when his [?] give scrapes
Put his mouth in many shapes.

Another week has pass'd and flown
And other thoughts and wishes form
And other thoughts of the Future and of those
Cherished in memory and in heart repose.

This moon, sweet Sabbath day
Light up my soul with happy ray
With adoration and with humble praise
To thee my thankful morning song I'll raise.

I love this peaceful quiet Sabbath morn
All nature silent and myself adorn
With flowers that fond remembrance bring
Its fragrance sweet from love's pure spring.

For tis not time, or sailing on the sea
Or clime, or change or what can be
Will steal from Friendship alter [altar?] a little part
Or loose a Silken cord from any heart.

There dwells my hopes of future happiness
When Dear Mother you may find a rest
From toilsome labour free, and in a land so fair
To spend the winter of your days all free from anxious care.

[The diary ends here. James follows this last entry with lists of the crew and passengers, so perhaps did not intend to add anything further.]

RETURN VOYAGE IN THE *ROYAL SHEPHERDESS*, 1851

[These entries were on loose pages at the back of the earlier diary.]

Tuesday, May 6

One of the wetest days known since I have been in the Colony, the full benefit of which I was doom'd to experience. This being the lastest day my stay on shore could be prolonged to (a report being generally circulated through Adelaide that the *Royal Shepherdess* was to leave Port this afternoon) at 9 oclock am I left my Lodging and sought a conveyance for myself and luggage to the Port of Embarkation. It was raining at this time, which induced me to seek a covered vehicle. I soon learnt that there was only two on the road, one a four Horse coach or rather Omnibus, and the other a Carriers Cart, the first of which I was too late for and the other to give me a lift in that was to be a great favour as passengers were seldom taken, being intended only for luggage and small parcels. After waiting a couple of hours at the house of an acquaintance I started in the luggage Cart and had not proceeded a quarter of a Mile before the Rain descended in torrents. Not being able to remove to the back of the Cart I caught the rain in front and from the Cover behind, running down my back from thence to the seat, wetting me in every part, most miserable, a more disagreeable ride I never had in my life. This state of things continued for the first four miles, to the first halfway house. I say to the first Halfway House as there are two called by that name, one at the distance of a Quarter of a mile from the other. They appear to make it a practice of stoping at the first they come to, which ever way they are travelling. They are distinguished by the New and the Old

Halfway house. The Old One has been built upwards of 12 years, From the heavy rain that had fallen during the last two days, the road was almost impassable and occupied us an hour to do the four miles. At the Halfway House was one of the Post Carts, into which after taking sundry nobliers of Brandy I jumped. These carts being built light and drawn by two Horses can make their way through the mud easier than any other conveyance. They are capable of carrying nine, but oftener, to oblige, a dozen. There is no restriction as to number, the practice adopted being to take all they can get. Arrived at the Port I immediately took Boat to the Ship, and there made an exchange of dry for wet clothes, riturned in the same Boat to awaited the arrival of the Capt. Dined at the Railway after [-] conveyed my [-] Boxes etc to Ship. To add to the unpleasantness of the whole my Bedding was found to be wet, with the knowledge that I must take it for better or worse and turn into it as it was, although suffering with a bad cough, there being not the slightest chance of drying them by fire. Retired early to Bed, feeling quite tired.

[Page cut at the top, some words missing]

Wednesday May 7

Arose tolerable refreshed from the slumbers of the past night feeling little or no ill effects from the weting of yesterday or damp Bedding. Engaged stowing away boxes getting things things to rights and helping others do the same with there's. All on board bussle and confusion, a move being intended to be made tomorrow. Had I have been worthy to have known so much time still remained, before we started, I would not have travelled one yard in the pelting Rain.

Thursday May 8th

Employed myself much as yesterday. Passengers and Luggage, with Provisions of all kinds arriving hourly Fowls, Pigs with Cow & Calf helping to form part of the motley group, and render the confusion still greater, noise and swearing without intermision, it would seem of a single five minutes. Having a purchase of one or two things to make on shore and an opportunity to go in one of our own Boats occurring, I imbraced it little dreaming how dear I should have to pay for being thus forward. The Carpenter, Butcher with Cook formed part of the crew, myself and another Passenger, with couple of sailors making up the number, we left the ship about 7 oclock, agreeing for all to meet at a certain Public House at 9 pm. The little business that engaged myself was soon dispatched and meeting with the Cook we both made for the Public House and discussed matters over a pot of Stout. 9 oclock came and we had only mustered four of our Party. Unfortunately at this time in came three friends of the Carpenter, who having had quite as much as they could do with themselves, insisted upon treating him. We were then showed into another little room, a private appartment, admittance only being given to those well known, friends of course, and great drinkers, characters well known to Polly Grey as supporters of the Commercial Inn. Polly was an old lag and had come to Australia from Van Diemans Land with a former Husband, her present one being the third and he almost a cipher, Polly herself filling the situations of Master and Mistress. She was always spoken of as a very flash woman. I [-] of common occurance. This information I had from the Carpenter who named her as being a friend of his and the House he always used. Had I have left by myself at the time of our making the exchange of appartments, I should have been on board at good hour, as also been able to procure a Boat. As it was, when I came to the determination to leave and go by myself, I found no waterman was to be had. All had left either for the Public House or their homes. I was therefore obligated to remain where I was or risk going to the Ship with them. Time thus passed away and from 12 untill half past 2 many were the moves made towards starting but ere that was gained the clock had warned for 3 am. Two of our Party was very drunk and only placed in the boat by the united efforts of those who, under any other circumstances, would have been thought in a situation just able to care of themselves. Arrived on board without accident comforting myself that the evenings amusement had learnt me a lesson not readily to be forgotten. I may also have name that when we reached our Boat it was found some person or persons had stollen our oars. These were however soon replaced by another pair being taken from one of the Boats belonging to a Ship part of whos crew was on shore, a fact known to the Friends of our Carpenter.

Friday May 9th

All hands preparing for the start, early part of morning engaged unmooring the vessel. Pilot on board by 10 oclock. At 4 pm was being towed by Steamer out of Harbour, amidst the Cheering of each Ships crews as we passed them. Anchored at the North Arm, where we are to remain it is said for two or three days. We had a very pleasant trip, it being a fine day and delightful weather. The arm of the sea extending inland from Snappers Point to the port is considered from 12 to 14 miles and is in width about the same as the Thames, I should guess varying from a half to three quarters of a mile. The light ship is in the open roadstead, and served as a guide for ships to anchor, on their first arrival. From thence they are taken by a pilot. The present Light Ship is an old French vessel, the *Ville de Bourdeaux* and was seazed by the English for smuggling.

That not being substantiated the trial was lost and cost the home Government 20 or 30,000£. The crew was boarded and lodged at Fordhams, the present Sturt Hotel, and incur'd a debt of 400£ which was never liquidated. The Sturt Hotel is at Adelaide and this occurance took place now eleven years ago.

Saturday May 10th

This comparatively a quiet day. The Ships Crew engaged setting up sails and Rigging. Provisions taken on board, few left the ship, the boat once only to the Port. Little or nothing being done by Passengers.

Sunday May 11

The only amusement to which the day will permit our having recourse is the Book. Numbers were thus engaged, and reading was evidently the favourite employment. None of the Passengers left the ship. Several spent the Sunday on Shore but those left yesterday. The head Clerk from Venn's with three other Gentlemen came in their Boat, and spent the afternoon with the Captain.

Monday May 12

Not so fine a day. Morning rather cold. Considerable quantity of Luggage arrived and Stores taken in. Passengers engaged making Boxes etc etc secure, preparing for a toss about, which all expect on being towed out to the Light Ship. This however is not expected before Wednesday from the unpropicious state of the weather.

Tuesday May 13th

In every respect the weather and movements on board the same as yesterday. Captain to the port with sailors to scull the Boat, two of whom were the worse for liquor before they returned to the Ship.

Wednesday May 14th

Morning cold but fine. Crew engaged raising anchor. Pilot came on board at 10 am. Were taken in Tow by the Steamer at 1pm and rounded the Light Ship at 5pm. Strong wind but not favouring our course. Tacked ship at [-] Heavy Sea on and vessel rolling violently. Many sick including myself. Ship makes much water. Pumps at work every two hours. It is hoped she will take up and not be so leaky in a few days.

Thursday May 15

Day fine, rather inclined to be cold, but no rain a favourable change of the wind and we are able to do our course, proceeding at 6 and 7 knotts per hour. Feel myself rather better in health, but far from being quite comfortable. A slight consolation that others are in the same predicament, not yet able to tackle the salt Horse, or remain below any length of time.

Friday May 16

Still favoured with fine weather and doing our course well. Hope to round Cape Lewin [Leeuwin] about Wednesday or Thursday next. Myself as also many of the Passengers are beginning to get their sea legs on.

Saturday May 17

Proceeding down Investagator Straits with favourable wind doing 8 Knotts. Ship still in a moist state, and a continual pumping kept up. Carpenter engaged repairing Pumps several times, one of them being particularly bad, and expected to give out every hour. Were it not for this unpleasant state of affairs, all would be comfortable.

Sunday May 18th

Strong head wind with heavy rain. The leakey state of our Ship is now fully tested. While we had the wind aft it was nothing to alarm, but being now against us, and the vessel pitching and every timber on the strain the leakage considerable increases, obliging us to keep the pump going every quarter of an hour, making 15 inches during that time, or about 42 feet per hour. To add to our unenviable situation one of the Pumps has refused to work three or four times. Were both of them thus to give out four hours would suffice to cause the disappearance of both crew and Ship. Divine Service performed between Decks in the Steerage for the first time, read by the Doctor, the Captain and two Ladies from the Cabin attending.

Monday May 19th

This morning we were informed that at Eleven oclock last night a consultation took place between our Skipper, Mate, Carpenter and Captain Fowler (passenger in the Cabin) when after an hours consideration, it was determined to return if possible to Adelaide. Had it not been for the number of Passengers on board the Vessel would have been lightened by a quantity of the copper being thrown over board and proceeded onwards. Our Captain at one part of the consultation had almost determined thus to act but the very dangerous state of the Ship and the consideration of the number of lives which it was too probable would be sacrificed induced the attempt to regain port Adelaide. A continuation of the wind in the. same quarter on our [banting ?] Ship favoured our return and we are proceeding fast toward the Land. When we turned the head of her again for Australia we had gone 100 miles having had a capital run. The water still increasing upon us, makes us all anxious once more to see Land.

Tuesday May 20th

Wind still continuous favourable, and for the past twenty-four hour we have being doing well. We are all anxiety to sight Kangaroo Island. This however would not be expected, with ever so good a run, for at least three days. All quiet and comfortable on board, nothing beyond the usual business and amusement of Ship life taking place.

Wednesday May 21

This day spent much like that of yesterday. Our principal amusement and never failing subject of discussion is the aggravating Pumps. They seem to work only just when they are in the humour, sometimes one and then the other giving out, causing us no little anxiety. The wind remains the same and we continue on our course back, with the same rapidity as when we were making from the land. Vessel rolling violently several times during the day capsizing every thing not lashed, breaking the Crockery and upsetting the tin ware. The Doctor stood at the Wheel for an hour, and is considered to be as good at the Helm as either of the sailors. This is very unusual and what I never saw done before.

Thursday May 22nd

In all respects spent much like many of the proceeding. This Evening land said to be seen from the mast Head.

Friday May 23rd

Sighted Kangaroo Island. The wind however being dead a Head of us we were the whole of this day tacking. Bouling [bailing?] Ship every hour. The Pumps afford us all the amusement desired, working them every quarter of an hour.

Saturday May 24

Rough morning. Strong Breeze in our teeth. Arrived at the Light Ship at 11am. Remained at anchor until 3 pm when we were taken in Tow by the Steam Tug, passing the North Arm at 2 past 4 and arriving at the Port at 6. Close along side us is the fine Barque *Carlton*.

Sunday 25 May

Dull morning and rather cold. Rain'd much at different times during the day. Did not leave the ship. Only one of our Party ventured upon Shore to Church or Chapel and that for the Morning Service. No Service held on board, nothing beyond the usual amusements attending Ship Life throughout the day.

Monday May 26

Ship's Company engaged securing Vessel to Wharf, removing Sails, and making the necessary preparation for men to commence unloading tomorrow morning, which it is understood is intended. Rain at intervals through the day.

Tuesday May 27

At 6 oclock this morning we were obliged to turn out as a Gang of a dozen sturdy fellows were come to commence unloading Cargo. The work was done by contract, which was taken by one a Mr Stone and I understood was to be completed for 70£. It is believed all will be out of the Vessel and she will be ready to be placed upon the slip by Friday or Saturday.

Wednesday May 28

Disturbed again this morning at dawn of Day. Everything is in such miserable confusion that there is no comfort up and less in the Hammock. Day cold and wet. Walked on Shore for short time before Breakfast. Bought loaf

[The diary finishes here.]

THE VOYAGE OF THE *ASIA*

Latitude and Longitude, Distance covered and Temperature.

24 Oct 1849 Left Plymouth
Wind west/southwest Course steering 8½ west
26 Oct
Course SW wind WSW Latitude 49.49 N
27 Oct
Course SW 48 miles this day Latitude 49 10 N Long 5 deg 22 W
Barometer 29.95 inches Thermometer 62 deg
28 Oct
S 70 N 30 miles L 49.2 N Long 5.50 B 30.50 T 61.50
29 Oct
Course S 50 deg W Miles 59 Lat 48.20 N Long 6.56 W
B 30.10 inches T 62.0
Lat 48 deg 19 N Long 7.10 W [Both same day. Witnessed shipwreck of a steamboat. Hove to to rescue crew and moveables. Lost about 20 miles.]
30 Oct
Course S 46 W Lat 48.4 N Long 8.56 W B 30.10 Thermometer 62
31 Oct
Course S 8 W Miles 143 Lat 45.58 Long 11.27 W B 29.90 T 59.50
1 Nov
Miles 156 Lat 43.34 Long 11.54 B 29.40 T 58.0
2 Nov
Course S 1½ points W Miles 163 Lat 41.4 N Long 12.56 B 29.40 inches T 58.0

3 Nov
Course S 14 deg W Miles 185 Lat 38.5 N Long 13.56 W
B 29.30 T 60.00
4 Nov
Course 1½ Pt W Miles 200 Lat 35.33 Long 12.37 W B 29.75 inches T 65.00
5 Nov
Course 48 deg W 160 miles Lat 33.47 N Long 14.37 B 30.10 T 67.00 Sighted P[orto] Santo W ½ S 34 miles
6 Nov
15 miles from Madeira Barometer 30.10 inches Thermometer 69 Santo Long 16.20 W Lat 32.58 N
8 Nov
Lat 30.22 N Long 18.43 W B 30.10 T 73.50
9 Nov
Course S 43 W Miles 155 Lat 28.29 Long 20.34 B 36.10 inches T 75.00
10 Nov
Course S 46 deg W Miles 169 Lat 26.12 N Long 22.35 B 29.90 T 75.80
11 Nov
Course S 42 deg W 105 miles Lat 24.54 Long 23.52 B 29.82 T 73.00
12 Nov
Course S 54 deg W 120 miles Lat 23.44 Long 25.38 B 30.00 T 72.50
13 Nov
Course S SW Lat 23.3 Long 26.12
14 Nov
Course S SW Lat 21.54 Long 26.40
15 Nov
Lat 19.44 N Long 26.35

16 Nov
Lat 17.6 Long 26.5
17 Nov
Lat 14.36 Long 25.30
18 Nov
Lat 13.1 Long 24.58
19 Nov
Lat 10.49 Long 24.13
20 Nov
Lat 8.49 Long 24.13
22 Nov
Lat 7.17 Long 24.28 W
23 Nov
Lat 5.49 Long 24.28
24 Nov
Lat 4.28 Long 24.45
25 Nov
Lat 3.27 Long 25.11
26 Nov - 10 Dec - no record of Latitude and Longitude
11 Dec
SE Lat 23.13 Long 24.34 8124 from Australia 2312 from the Cape

No further record of Latitude and Longitude

CAPTAIN, OFFICERS AND CREW OF THE *ASIA*

Taken from James Broom's list in his diary

Cap. Roskill	[John Roskell]	
Doctor	Mr Catlet	
Mr Silk	1st Mate	
Wm Henry Faithfull	2 "	
Hastings Baker	3 "	
Matthew Box	4 "	Transgressed and put out of office for 2 weeks, obliged to be with sailors
Masters	Patterson	Apprentice
	Nealds	5 Mate
	De Mole	Midshipman
	Hose	"
	Harland	Apprentice
	* Bonifant	Apprentice
Thos Brightstone	remaining at Plymouth	

Ships Crew	
Joseph Beenden	Boatswain
John Brockbank	Ships Carpenter
Geo Green	
John & Will Haray	
Jas Gray	
John Whitehead	
Jas Harper	

John Bepper	
Saml Williams	
Tho. Lowen	
Peter McDermot	
Daniel Lockarte	
Thos James	Sailmaker
Walter Stocks	
John Fearon	
Ed'n Beesley	
W Henry Colestone	
Tho's Coldwell	
Thos Pellem	Passengers Cook
Thos Richards	Cooks Mate

Sailors	
Huntington	working out his passage and serv't to the male adults. Tailor by trade and making a good thing of it, at work all day long.
Thos Holt	working out his passage Serv't to females & [?] men for Middle Hatch
James Cately	Steward to the Captain
Charles Norcott	(alias James Dicks) Serv't to Steward and keeper of the Pigs, Sheep & Poultry Part Working out Passage Paid 10£
Peter Lasoux	Cook for Captain & Ship's Company

* *The South Australian Register* Tuesday February 19, 1850, under "Miscellaneous Shipping", gives an account of the loss of Thomas Bonifant, a midshipman on board the *Asia*, on 30 December. He slipped overboard while unfurling the fore-topmast studding sail. It was a very dark and wet night, and, though boats were sent after him, and every effort made, he was not seen again.

PASSENGERS ON THE *ASIA*

The list of passengers and notes are taken from the diary, from the *The South Australian Register* Tuesday, February 19, 1850, and information from the South Australian Maritime Museum.

Port Adelaide

Mr & Mrs Barker: Linen draper, acted as auctioneer of Thomas McKeckney's perishable goods. One passenger, unnamed, but possibly Mr Barker, was a linen draper according to James, and had part of his stock with him. He was not long married, his wife being some years his junior. He was a member of the Independent Church, "and one of those little quiet men peculiar to the cloth". There were two other drapers, also bound to Adelaide, "but hope not to be obliged to follow the old Trade". 9 November.

Charles Broadrill: From Warminster, Wiltshire, a friend of James Broom. Was accompanied to Exeter by his father. James gives his surname as Brodribb. There is no record of the name Broadrill in the Warminster Museum, nor elsewhere in Wiltshire in the 1851 Census, but Brodribb (with slight variations in spelling) occurs frequently, both at the time of the diary and at the present day. Pigot's and Slater's Directories for Warminster between 1830 and 1852 include Chas. Brodribb, Ironmonger & Leather Seller, also J D & U Brodribb, Grocer and Wine Merchant, both of Market Place.

Miss Harriet Bromley

James Brown: [Broom] the diarist.

William Brown: Quarrelled with George Henry Ryan after drinking rum and ale. The Captain ordered him to his cabin, under guard. Took part in concert 24 November

George Carpenter: Stayed in the same hotel in Plymouth as James and Charles.

Mr Richard Crabb: Veterinarian, and Mrs Elizabeth Crabb, with children Caroline, Emily, Benjamin and John

Mr & Mrs Doswell and three children

Mr Ed Dutton: Farmer and brewer and Mrs Dutton, with three children. Eliza Dutton was linked with Charles Willimott in the poem 22 December.

Frederick Ediston, also recorded as Elliston and, in the diary, as Ellison. Was known to Thomas McKeckney, and waited on him in his illness.

William Finnis: Took part in concert 24 November.

Mrs Sarah A Francis: Mr Matthew Box, acting 3rd Officer, was demoted by the Captain for going into her cabin when he should have been on duty. 10 November

Miss Caroline Harris: Linked with Cornelius Smith, in poem 22 December, but rejected him.

Edward Hodson

Miss Mary Jeffrey

Edward Johnson

Arthur Markhill: Took part in concert 24 November

Charles Matthews and three children

Thomas McKeckney: Died of consumption 7 December aged 20 and was buried at sea. He had a mother and sister living at Bow,

London, and left them to go to Launceston, Van Diemen's Land [Tasmania] for his health. His brother was living there. He was of middle stature, according to James.

Charles Norcott: alias James Dicks Plasterer and farm labourer. Also on the Crew List, part working his passage, paid £10

Richard and William Rowed, brothers

Frederic Salter: Took part in concert 24 November

Cornelius Smith: Linked with Caroline Harris in poem 22 December, but was rejected by her.

Edward Sunter

Miss Isabella Sunter

Robert Whitten or Whitton

William Charles Willimott: Ship broker and stock agent. Took part in concert 24 November.

Henry Yateman

Port Phillip

W Alexander

Mr & Mrs Bean with six children

Mr & Mrs Cocks

Mrs Gertrude Dunn: Took part in concert 24 November.

Mr & Mrs Hawkes: Married about ten days before departure. 8 November. Owners of piano played one evening by Mrs Laseward and the Misses Neald. Mr Hawkes took part in concert 24 November. Mrs Fanny Hawkes died 13 January of effusion on the brain. On the Port Phillip passenger list, but James said they were going to Sydney.

Mr & Mrs Laseward and one child. (Lakewood) Mr Laseward led the services on Sundays and the funeral service for baby Mary Ann Mumby, who died on 22 November. Mrs Laseward played the piano one evening and took part in the concert 24 November.

Martha Longhurst: Linked with Thomas Winterton in poem 22 December

Mr & Mrs Lowe

Lewin McKenzie & James McKenzie, brothers. James McKenzie and Thyrza Neald subjects of song 17 December. James helped Mr McKenzie to repack his box of clothes.

Charlotte Matthews

James E B Mumby: Brother of Mr Mumby

Mr & Mrs Mumby and five children Their 4 month old baby, Mary Ann, died of mesenteric disease 22 November and was buried at sea the next day. Mr Lasewood took the service.

Mrs Nealds and two children Mrs Nealds and the Misses Neald took part in the concert on 24 November. The Misses Neald also played the piano one evening. One of the sisters was Miss W Neald. The other sister was named Thyrza, and was the subject, with James McKenzie, of a song 17 December. A Mr Nealds was in the Officers and Crew List as 5th Mate.

John Richardson

George Henry Ryan: Quarrelled with William Brown after drinking rum and ale. The Captain ordered him to the poop, under guard.

James Shaw

Mary Ann Shaw

Mr & Mrs Smith and one child: Mrs Smith was James's partner in Quadrille.

Peter Thompson

Thomas Turner: Linked with Kate Rooney in poem 22 December.

John R Thomson

Madeline Vallant

George Ward

Alfred Ward

Thomas Winterton: Took part in the concert 24 November. Linked with Martha Longhurst in poem 22 December.

Sydney

Thomas Bach

Ann Burrows & Mary Burrows: One of them linked with William Henry Faithfull, 2nd Mate, in poem 22 December.

Joseph Cadogan

Mary Ann Chilcott

Maria Chilcott

John Davison

John Delday

Mrs Emma Garsed: Took part in concert 24 November.

John Grig

John Haskew

Mary Haskew

Walter Harris

Mr & Mrs Little

Mr & Mrs Levitt

William Meadows

Mrs Norris & Ellen Norris: Took part in concert 24 November.

Jonas Ollson Ole Jonas Ollson, from Norway, according to James's passenger list.

Robert Pain

Edward Row

Kate Rooney: Irish, Linked with Thomas Turner in poem 22 December.

Henry S[olide]r

Alex Sidey

Andrew Simpson: Colonel, Leader of concert 17 November, took part in concert 24 November, author of song about James McKenzie and Thyrza Neald 17 December

William Tillman

William Thomas

Thomas Webb

William Wernham

Francis Woolbert

Philip White: Last situation was at Buckingham Palace. Going to Australia for his health.

CAPTAIN, OFFICERS AND CREW OF THE *ROYAL SHEPHERDESS*

Taken from the entries in James Broom's diary.

Captain	John Bell	
Carpenter	)	All three went on shore, to meet at a public house - the Commercial Inn? James had matters of business to deal with and was to join them there, to return to the ship with them.
Butcher	) 8 May	
Cook	)	
Mate		
Doctor	21 May	"The Doctor stood at the Wheel for an hour, and is considered to be as good at the Helm as either of the sailors. This is very unusual and what I never saw done before."

PASSENGERS ON THE *ROYAL SHEPHERDESS*

The list of passengers is taken from *The South Australian Register* 9 May 1851:

Master: Bell

In the cabin:

Mr & Mrs Bland

Miss Bland & servant

Mr & Mrs White

Mr & Mrs Amsberg

Mr Fowler [In the entry for 19 May referred to as Captain Fowler]

Mr Coode

Mr Alderson

Mr Golling

Mr Rock (surgeon)

In the intermediate:

Mrs Bonning & family

Mrs Lehril

Mr & Mrs Wylie & child

Mr Powell

Mr Simpson

Mr Younghusband

[The cargo lists for both the *Asia* and the *Royal Shepherdess* include the firm of Younghusband & Co. They imported 35 barrels on the *Asia* - the list does not state the contents - and exported 20 bales of wool on the *Royal Shepherdess*.]

Mr Thorne

<u>Steerage</u>:

Mr McGlen
Mr Rawlls
Mr Hooper
Mr Dowling
Mr Gothard
Mr Bunn
Mr Hanbury
Mr Rilsey
Mr Archer
Mr Lye
Mr Kingstone
Mr Kanter
Mr Nicksons (two)
Mr Thomas
Mr Brown [James Broom, the diarist]
Mrs Coppin & child

CARGOES

Lists taken from *The South Australian Register*

Tuesday February 19, 1850 Shipping Intelligence

Imports Cargo of the *Asia*

4 casks, J H Lucking; 4 cases, Robert White & Co; 100 hhds, Alex Thomson; 9 cases, 12 bales, Miller & Lucking; 6 trunks, 1 case, R F McGeorge; 1 case, Blyth Brothers; 2 cases, 1 cask Order; 15 cases, W. Barker; 3 cases, A. Thomson; 40 hhds, R. Parker; 100 casks, Montefiore & Co; 21 casks, R. Lambell; 1 case, J. Johnson; 40 hhds, 135 battens, C. & F. J. Beck; 35 barrels, Younghusband & Co; 5 pipes, A. Scott; 20½ tierces, N. P. Le Bair; 1 bale, 11 cases, 13 casks, 2 crates, 1 bundle, 200 camp ovens, and 230 covers, 80 mould boards, Blyth Brothers; 16 casks, 6 hhds, 92 kegs, 1½ boxes, 126 bundles 255 iron pots, 36 axle arms, 194 pairs brushes, 49 grindstones, 9 casks, J. Henry; 7 cases, 1 bale, Miller & Luckings.

Friday May 9 1851 Shipping Intelligence

Exports Cargo of the *Royal Shepherdess*

9 bales wool. Were. Todd and Co; 9 bales wool, J & M Colville; 46 bales wool, W. Peacock; 6 bales wool, J Morphett; 24 bales wool, J Stilling & Co; 5 bales wool, J. Bennett; 175 bales wool, A. L. Elder & Co; 86 bales wool, John Roberts; 27 bales wool, E Little; 20 bales

wool, Younghusband & Co; 24 bales wool, Aylwin; 21 casks tallow, J Stilling & Co; 9 casks tallow, 1 package leather, A L Elder & Co; 1 case model mine, C & F J Beck; 1 box specimens, S R Hall; 1 box, C Everitt; 4 boxes R Rhodda; 131 blocks copper, P Levi; 1,796 ingots 277 tiles, 1,100 ingots 63 tiles copper, John Roberts; 5,173 cakes 12,420 tiles copper, South Australian Mining Association; 180 bags copper ore, 128 bags regulus, J Hayes; 9 casks tallow, P Levi; 1 cask hardware, W Blyth; 1 box apparel Acraman & Co; 6,401 trensils, 21 cwt old copper, J Bell.

SOURCES AND ACKNOWLEDGEMENTS

Art Gallery of South Australia, Adelaide
British Library
British Library Newspaper Library
Dewey Museum, Warminster, Wiltshire, Mr G A Hardy, Hon: Curator
Merseyside Maritime Museum, Liverpool
National Maritime Museum, Greenwich
South Australian Genealogy and Heraldry Society, Inc.
State Library of South Australia, Adelaide
South Australian Maritime Museum, Adelaide
State Records of South Australia, Adelaide
West Devon Area Record Office, Plymouth

Stuart and Sheila Braidford, graphics, proof-reading and layout.
Shelagh Fitzarthur, typing the first draft of the transcription
Victor Jellings, drawing of a typical barque
Alison J Maddock, research
Brian and Ruth Pettey, research
John and Dalece Pope, South Australia, information and illustrations
Ray Wilson, transcribing the first draft onto the computer
Stephen Wright, research

Publications:

Almanack, Murray, Adelaide, 1850

Highways & Byways in Wiltshire, Hutton, Edward, Macmillan & Co., 1919

Historic Buildings of South Australia, National Trust of South Australia, Axiom Publishers, 1995

History of Warminster, Daniell, John J, Warminster, 1879, 3rd edition 1985

History of Wiltshire, Watkin, Bruce, Phillimore, 1989

Log of Logs, Vol: 1, Nicholson, Ian, Roebuck, Queensland, 1993

South Australia, Harcus, William, ed: Sampson Low & Co, London, 1876

South Australian Register, 19 February 1850 & 9 May 1851

Sophy Under Sail, Taylor, Irene C, Hodder & Stoughton, 1969

Warminster in the Twentieth Century, Lane, Celia & White, Pauline, Warminster History Society, 1999

William Wood's Diary, Pennington, Peter, Ardnamona Publishers, 2002

Special thanks are due to Stuart Braidford, without whose help this book would not have been possible in its present form.

INDEX

Names of people found only in the Crew and Passengers Lists with no other information are not included in the Index. Please see these lists.